Come Walk With Me
Across The Years

Beginning with 1922

by
Marjorie Larson Sinks

Come Walk With Me Across The Years is an adventure story of the 1920's through the 1990's. It is an autobiography yet it relates life as it was for many Americans during those decades. It recalls struggles, joys, strengths, weaknesses and achievements. More than one thousand notable events and persons are included as history in the making.

Published by
Centennial Publishing House
1071 Centennial Drive
Loveland, CO 80538
USA

Printed by Pioneer Impressions
Fort Collins, CO 80524

Cover design by Peter Pohle

Library of Congress Catalog Number 94-94167
ISBN 0-9641708-0-9 9.95

This story is dedicated to every reader
and to friends who have
walked with me across the years.

About the Author

More than 200 articles by Marjorie Larson, B.A., M.A. have been published. She has written for radio, television and films. "Encounter At Midnight" was selected by Robert Walker as a best story for his book *"The Gift of His Heart"*, Fleming H. Revell Company, Publishers.

Contents

❧

ONE

Smart Women
Don't Have Babies

"It's a girl."

"I didn't want a girl!" Dad protested when I was born that August morning in 1922. "Girls are too hard to raise. You got to watch them every minute or they're liable to disgrace the family."

Dad's remark made Mother sad but she wasn't surprised. He had told her several times that he hoped she had another boy and not a girl.

"She's got blue eyes," Mother stated defensively. "Come and look at her." Dad's eyes were blue. Mother's were dark brown, almost black.

"All babies got blue eyes," he answered.

Mother propped herself on an elbow. She was weak from a night of strenuous labor but she lovingly stroked the baby girl lying at her bosom. She asked Dad, "What do you think we ought to name her?"

"I don't care what you call her," Dad replied. "You can name her what you please. I don't want to name any girl."

Dad, usually pretty cool, was in an irritable mood. He had been awake all night trying, as best he could, to comfort Mother and to follow her instructions.

My parents lived in a three room house on ten acres of rented land. At five that morning, Dad had fetched the neighbor lady, Mrs. Thatch, to help as midwife. Then when his unmarried brother Bill came by, Dad sent him running for Dr. Martin. There wasn't anything unusual about my birth and fortunately the doctor arrived in time to deliver me.

That was better than Dr. Martin had done on a cold night nineteen months earlier when my brother Bob was born in the same house. Bob arrived two hours before the Doctor did. Mom and Dad were scared because the doctor was late in coming but Grandma was there and she helped deliver my brother. She had borne thirteen children herself at home and knew a lot about having babies. She was blind in one eye and negligent about details of cleanliness but she was always willing to help with a delivery.

Dad kept a fire roaring in the pot belly stove. Mother probably watched every move he and Grandma made. Mother was a perfectionist and she wanted to be sure her newborn was given meticulous care. She was nervous about Grandma handling him.

Even before his son was an hour old Dad announced, "We'll name him after my father, Samuel Robert Summers, and we'll call him Bob."

Grandma was pleased. "Pop will like that," she said. Grandma was about to cut the cord with some scissors when Dad exclaimed, "Don't you dare cut it! We'll wait for the doctor."

Grandma was flustered. She argued that the cord ought to be cut right away. "The baby is in danger of getting too much blood," she said.

Mother agreed. However, Dad remained firm. "We'll wait for the doctor! Even if we have to wait until night!"

Grandma retorted, "I guess I know as much about babies as any doctor does." They waited anyhow. Mother swears the baby grew crimson from too much blood seeping from the afterbirth and she became pale from losing too much. She was scared. Still, everybody survived.

When Dr. Martin arrived he checked the baby boy's breathing and then he cut the cord. He dropped Argyrol in Bobby's eyes. That was a medication used to prevent eye disease. After carefully examining Bob he examined Mother.

The doctor wrote my brother's name in a book, the date of birth, birthplace and my parents' names, Frank and Rose Summers. Dad proudly told the doctor that Bob was born one day before his twenty-third birthday and that his wife, Rose, was nineteen. Dr. Martin said he'd hold that information two weeks before registering the birth. If unfortunately the baby died before then he wouldn't register it.

Most babies were born at home during the 1920's just as they had been for centuries. Usually relatives and friends were in attendance. Having a baby at home cost only what the doctor charged, perhaps twenty dollars. That was much cheaper than going to the hospital where a delivery might cost a hundred dollars. In the hospital you'd have to stay at least ten days. Childbirth was treated like a serious illness there. Only the rich could afford that kind of care.

After the doctor left, Mother raised up from her bed and noticed Grandma wiping some fluid with her hand from her runny, blind eye. Then she picked up the newborn boy. Mother about flipped. What if her mother-in-law got some of that goop on her son! The thought was unbearable!

Immediately Mother informed Dad that he should tell his mother they didn't need her help any longer and she could go home. Thanks for coming but probably Pop needed her. Please let Pop and the rest of the family know that the baby was O.K. Pop would be proud to hear that he had a grandson named after him.

Grandma departed quickly in her horsedrawn carriage. She probably was indignant at no longer being wanted and never forgot Mother's rapid dismissal. However, she didn't hold a grievance. Plenty of other women needed her help delivering babies.

Mother and her baby.

Rosie was too fussy, anyhow. All the family knew it. Nobody could please her. Grandma did not attend the entry into this world of Mother's second and third children.

When I was born the doctor left without a name for me. My parents didn't have a name picked for a girl. Dad told the doctor that Mother would let him know when she decided what to call me.

When I was a day old Uncle Mike, my mother's brother, came to visit us.

"Frank is real upset that we got a girl," Mother told him. "He says I have to name her and I don't have a name picked out. I was sure we'd have a boy."

Mike loved children, even girls. He had none of his own and wished Aunt Mary would get pregnant.

"There's a new song out that's very pretty and it's getting real popular," Uncle Mike said. "Maybe you can name her after that song."

My uncle had a good voice. He sang, "Margie, my little Margie, I'm always thinking of you Margie…."

Mother remarked, "That's pretty. You think we ought to call her Margie?"

"I think so. And you can give her the name of your favorite niece as her middle name."

Mother asked, "Marie?"

"Yes. Margie Marie. That goes good with Summers."

Mother smiled, then requested, "Sing another line."

"Sure. You are my inspiration Margie. I'll tell the world I love you. Don't forget your promise to me."

He stopped. "I've forgotten the rest of it."

"Well, I like it," Mother remarked. "Sounds good. I guess we'll call her Margie. Frank don't care."

"One of these days, when you're up and out of that bed," Uncle Mike said, "We'll be singing and dancing again!"

Mother laughed. "Me? With two babies? That's not likely!"

"You just wait and see!" Uncle Mike replied. "We were a winning team on the dance floor before you married Frank and we can be a winning team again!"

Uncle Mike was witty. Mother cherished the attention her brother gave her and had given her through the years, even though they had been separated much of the time. Mike and Mother looked a lot alike. Dark eyes, dark hair, and Italian-French features. Dad was as fair as they were dark.

"Why is Frank so upset over having a girl?" Mike asked.

"Well, he thinks she's likely to bring disgrace to the family. He's a very proud person. He just couldn't stand it if a daughter of his got pregnant out of wedlock."

Mike agreed there was a danger.

"Women have changed a lot during the last ten or twenty years," he said. "When our mother was a girl, women were much more modest. They didn't show off like they do these days."

"We've not really changed!" Mother defended. "We're still as good as we ever were!"

"Oh yeah?" Mike questioned. "You gotta admit a lot of women are becoming bossy and rebellious."

Mother laughed. "Aunt Mary?" she suggested.

"Well, not exactly," Uncle Mike replied. "But some girls are just plain flappers. Have you seen the scanty clothes they're wearing on the streets these days?"

"I've been too busy having babies," Mother said. Then she added, "Women are just trying to prove we're worth something."

"Yeah? Well, they claim the Miss America contest held in Atlantic City last year was meant to help women. Supposed to elevate them. Show their beauty and make them independent. I think it's leading them on the road to ruin."

"Frank fears what our daughter might be like when she grows up," Mother said.

As he left the house Uncle Mike remarked, "I hope she grows up to be as good as the song she's named after."

Dad had told Mother before they were married that he didn't want men joking about her like they did about some women. He said, "Rosie, I don't want you to wear short, tight dresses or long pants. I don't want you to cut your hair and I wish you wouldn't marcel it. And I don't like make-up." Rosie just listened and didn't answer.

"I married you because you've been a good woman," he said. "And I want you to stay that way."

Ralph, Margie and Bob, 1925

Ralph, my younger brother, came along sixteen months after I was born. By that time Mother was well experienced in delivery, taking care of babies and doing housework.

Our shack, as Mom and Dad called our house, had wood floors which Mother scrubbed daily. From early childhood I remember hearing people say you could eat off her floors. That could have been possible if you wanted to eat on newspaper. Mother always spread newspapers on the floor after she scrubbed it. We didn't have carpeting during those days but we did have several throw rugs, also covered with newspapers. Mother spread newspapers on the table, too, to keep the oilcloth clean.

The ink used in newspapers was more permanent at that time and didn't rub off. That was a great advantage.

Mother had her hands full raising us children, trying to keep us clean, well fed and healthy. Dad was away from home much of the time and Mother spent a lot of hours alone with us. She never seemed to stop working, however, except to sleep or to talk to us children. Undoubtedly, we were the center of her life.

Among my fondest recollections of Mother is her lying in bed with us and having us repeat family names. "Uncle Harvey, Uncle Sam, Uncle Mike, Uncle Richard, Aunt Blanche, Grandma, Grandpa…" There were dozens of relatives. It probably took a half hour to get through the list. She also taught us to pray, "Now I lay me down to sleep…" which ended with God blesses for everyone.

Mother wiggled our toes and repeated, "This little piggy went to market, this little piggy stayed home, this little piggy had roast beef and this little piggy had none. This little piggy cried 'wee, wee, wee,' all the way home." We loved it and the toe wiggling rhyme became a family tradition.

Mother also taught us tricks such as patting your head and rubbing your tummy at the same time. She could touch the tip of her nose with her tongue and encouraged us to do it. Only Bobby succeeded.

Bob was gentle and generous. When only three years old he assumed responsibility for us two younger ones when Mother worked outdoors doing such things as laundry. Mother tells of a time that she heard Ralph crying. When she reached him, however, he was quiet. Bob was kneeling over his baby brother and jiggling his bed. Bob's shirt tail was in the baby's mouth so he could chew on it and not cry. Ralph was pampered and he cherished every moment of it. He was a blond curly-headed darling, the last-to-be baby.

Three babies in less than three years compelled Dad to make the authoritative demand that she must never have any more children. It was up to Mother to see that there weren't. Mother was puzzled as to how she could cooperate but determined to comply. Anyway, she was beginning to feel humiliated by a sister-in-law who never got pregnant and boasted about it.

"Smart women don't have to have kids," the in-law said in family gatherings when only women were present. Then, when Mother's back was turned and was out of ear shot, that relative whispered, "Rose is like a rabbit – belly filled with a baby." At least that is what another relative meekly reported to Mother.

I came from a gossipy family. Mother, in turn, told me that relatives said that my aunt couldn't get pregnant because she had had too many men. Whether it was a catty remark or the truth, I'll never know. Later in life, however, that aunt told me she wished she could have had a child.

Mother resorted to various methods of birth control such as gold hooks, inserts of various sorts, salves, herbal remedies and potions, all of which were ineffective. These were things she told me when I was old enough to know the facts of life. The devices undoubtedly helped, or matters might have been worse. Mama said that Dad never cooperated. and more times than three she visited some illegal operator who employed health threatening proceedures that resulted in miscarriage. Those experiences haunted Mother through the years.

Being a father didn't keep Dad home but it kept Mother there. Dad had four unmarried brothers with whom he "hung out" at times, especially on Friday or Saturday night. Dad loved to gamble and helped run a gambling table. He always said he was going to make a lot of money gambling but it is doubtful he did. He pretty well broke even, however.

"The Boys," as my Dad and his brothers were called, weren't atheists but neither were they religious like their father. Grandpa was a very strict Christian. For some reason, however, his code was not matched by his sons. His daughters, however abode by his beliefs and became "church girls," the term used for females who attended church regularly. Although their brothers didn't attend neither did they disappove. Undoubtedly The Boys felt that religion would help keep their sisters out of the reach of prowling men.

The Jazz era occurred when I was a small child. A new style of American music developed in syncopated rhythm from the blues to ragtime.

The Jazz era coincided with the Great Prohibitiion. These were years during which the government forbade the manufacture, transportation and sale of alcoholic liquors. For some people prohibition seemed to turn drinking into a challenging sport. They found it fascinating to produce their own home brew, mainly a slightly fermented beer, or to try to buy contrabanded beverages.

I remember Dad making home brew when I was about six years old. He even let me taste it. My brothers claim I liked it. But then, I would never have told Dad I didn't. I thought too highly of him to disagree with him. By that time I think Dad had decided I was OK despite my being a girl. I can remember nothing to the contrary. If he ever worried that I might get pregnant out of wedlock I never knew it, except that Mother told me. Anyway, most parents didn't talk to their children about those kinds of things. To me, Dad expressed confidence and pride.

My mother and dad tolerated each other but neither one found life as happy as he or she had hoped it would be. They fought quite a lot. However, divorce was never suggested. The thought wasn't allowed. The word itself was like a curse word, uttered only by angry adults or naughty boys.

Mother was orphaned at age five when her mother died. She dreamed that marriage would fulfil her fantasies and provide total security. It didn't.

Mother treated me, even as a child, as a friend and confidant. Those qualities, however, did not fully compensate for idiosyncrasies which fractured the ties that should bind.

TWO

ह

We Had A Cow
Named Bossie

During the 1920's when I was born, America had a spectacular economic boom. Jobs, especially for laborers, were plentiful in Kansas City, my home town. Dad switched from one job to another until his third child was born. He was quite an ambitious fellow and, to use his expression, wanted to get ahead. He was short in stature, only five feet four inches, but tall in ambition.

Like many other working men who lacked technical skills or higher education, Dad wasn't much concerned about international affairs. He felt that the world was too big for him to give much thought to it. Only the educated and the rich had reason to be involved in world affairs. He was too busy eking out a living and solving his own problems to think about world government, big business and the like. However, he did devour the newspaper every day and he voted in the elections as a staunch Democrat.

Dad worked at a steel mill, then at a paper mill. After that he conducted a trolley car and later on he drove a truck. On the side, he farmed the small plot where we lived. He raised vegetables, mainly corn, beans, potatoes, tomatoes and cucumbers. He had a cow named Bossie that provided milk, and a horse named Bud that pulled a plow. We kids also rode Bud at times.

Mother and Dad raised chickens and a pig. My uncles helped butcher the pig and Mother preserved the meat by salting, smoking or canning. Mother wrung the necks of many chickens, plucked their feathers, removed the entrails and cut them in pieces which she fried in hot fat. Yum!

Dad had a hound dog or two most of the time and Mother detested them. She accused him of using them for dog fights and for racing but he denied it and said they were used only for hunting and protection.

We kids couldn't get close to some of those dogs. They were so angry. At times when Dad brought them home they had bloody gouges in their flesh and Dad had to "doctor" them.

I do know that Dad did use dogs for hunting because he'd come home with wild rabbits that the dogs had rounded up and Dad had shot. He also brought 'possums. Mother fried the former and rendered grease from the latter. We ate the rabbits with gusto and during winter nights Mother rubbed grease from the 'possums on our chests to protect us from getting colds.

One time after she rendered 'possum cracklings, she poured the grease in a jar and put the cracklings in a bowl on the table. She intended to dump the cracklings but before she was able to do it we three kids ate every morsel. To Mother that was sickening, like eating skunk, but to us kids they tasted great!

Mother started feeding table food to her babies when we were only a few months old, such as mashed potatoes, gravy, sweet potatoes, apple sauce and cornmeal mush. She nursed us at her breast until she got pregnant again and could no longer do it. All of us were "good eaters." Mother taught us to eat every bite on our plates. Nothing could be left. To clean our plate was the law.

She baked pies, cookies and cakes quite frequently but she seldom made candy. My parents bought flour, sugar, apples, potatoes and similar staples in one hundred pound quantities and stored them in the cellar where nothing froze or got too hot. Vegetables from our garden were stored there, too. The greatest enemy was mice. Dad set many a trap and caught many a mouse. I can still hear my Mother screeching as she emptied the traps.

The cellar also became a refuge during tornados. Mother was "scared to death" of tornados and she scurried us kids into the cellar when strong winds whipped across the fields and the skies darkened.

Our first home did not have running water or indoor plumbing. Water was drawn from a well on our property. Dad also collected rainwater in large drums outdoors just in case the well went dry or became frozen.

One task we kids had was to draw water from the well. At times we would pump hard on the handle but the water wouldn't rise. If Dad saw us struggling he shouted, "You have to prime the pump! How many times do I have to tell you?" He'd come to the well, pour some water down the shaft and pump hard on the handle. Gushes would rise.

For water to wash clothes, Dad carried bucketfuls from a nearby creek. He dumped the water, somewhat polluted, into a large pot kept outdoors and under which he built a fire. Mother added lye to the water which encouraged scum to rise. Then she skimmed the surface and added the clothes. She washed everything by hand on a washboard and used bars of homemade soap.

Before doing the laundry Mother sorted every article according to color. Whites were washed first, light colors next and dark colors last. The same tub of suds was used for all. Some clothing had dyes in them that weren't fast and the colors ran in the washwater. Mother had to make sure those articles were washed in a separate basin.

Two tubs of rinse water were used for rinsing clothes. One had bluing in it. That was a liquid used to counteract yellowing and to brighten garments. The rinse water sometimes had to be dumped since it got quite soapy after several uses.

When articles didn't come clean enough to suit Mother she boiled them in clean water, especially white things. She soaked clothing overnight that had resistant stains.

Mother liked to brag that she hung the cleanest line in town. She probably did and also the straightest, which meant that towels were hung next to towels, pants next to pants and sheets by sheets. Mother was chagrined to think that a neighbor might see her lines mixed with articles of different types. It seems that neighboring women competed in hanging the most beautiful line.

In the wintertime Mother hung most of her washings outdoors where they would freeze and yet amazingly get quite dry. And stiff. To finish the drying process she would hang the clothing on lines indoors and on furniture.

Every Monday was washday, no matter what. Tuesday was ironing day all day long. Our ironing board did not have legs but was stretched between chairs. The iron was heated on the stove, which used wood and coal.

For supper on Mondays we always had beans, pork and cornbread. Other days had similarly planned meals.

Quite often Mother made salmon croquettes. Canned salmon was cheap. Mother baked biscuits every morning and made all our light bread during those years.

We made toast by putting slices of bread in the oven of the cook stove. We had a waffle iron that was heated on top of the stove. The curling iron (yes, we had one despite Dad not wanting Mother to marcel her hair) was heated on the stove, too. We didn't have any electrical appliances.

One of the first purchases Dad made for Mother was a Singer sewing machine powered by a foot treadle. Mother never had a sewing lesson but she sewed all our baby clothes and made much of our clothing as we grew up. Ten or fifteen cents worth of cloth was enough to make me a dress.

We took our baths on Saturday night. The wash tub that hung outdoors was brought indoors and placed near the stove. Enough water was heated in pans to fill the tub halfway. Our soap was homemade and was strong with lye. Dad was the first to bathe and wash his hair. Mother was next. We kids were shoved into the bedroom and warned that we were never to peek while our folks were bathing. We didn't.

Finally we kids bathed, according to age. That made Bob first, me second and Ralph third.

Dad shaved with a straight razor. It had a long knife-like blade. He sharpened it on a strop which is a wide leather band. Frequently when he shaved he cut a nick in his face. After the single edge safety razor came into production, Dad was rescued from nicks and blood. So were ladies, like my Mother, who dared shave their legs and armpits.

Mother and Dad took us on the trolley car to Montgomery Ward and Sears. They bought us one dollar pairs of shoes. Mother paid ten cents a yard for drygoods to make shirts and dresses. Mother bought silk stockings. Ever so often she bought a new girdle for holding them up. Mother always had a round tummy and needed a girdle.

Our favorite store in downtown Kansas City was Woolworth's 5 and 10 at 12th and Main. We got chili hot dogs and root beer for ten cents. More than a thousand Woolworth 5 and 10 cent stores were in existence in the United States in the 1920's and J. C. Penney, by 1929, had more than a thousand stores. The era of advertising and slogans had begun and chain stores forged ahead with a vengeance.

A lot of people, such as farmers, couldn't get to the big city stores very often. Their need for supplies caused the creation of mail order stores, such as Sears Roebuck. A customer could order merchandise by mail from a catalog. People in town could also place orders and pick them up at the store.

Mom and Dad frequently ordered from a catalog and we waited at the store for our order to come down the chute, which was a channel through which items glided from storage to pick-up. I especially remember the long lines at Christmas time. We'd have to wait a half hour just to receive our order.

Although my parents demonstrated love by purchasing nice things for us and taking us shopping with them, I can never remember my parents kissing us or telling us they loved us. However, my mother hugged us sometimes. Neither of their families was demonstrative with affection. Their parents had so many children that they directed little attention toward any one. They fed them, kept them clothed, instructed and reprimanded them.

The strongest remembrance of love demonstrated to me was when I was a pre-schooler and an elderly man, Mr. Jack, stopped by our house for short visits. I'd crawl upon his lap and he'd rock me as we talked and laughed.

Several months before my fifth birthday Mother told me, "Margie, you must never sit on Mr. Jack's lap again. You are a big girl now. Big girls – good girls – don't sit on men's laps." The next time Mr. Jack came I ran from him. I was scared. My parents lauded my reaction. Mr. Jack undoubtedly was puzzled.

Dad warned my brothers, "Don't you ever touch your sister!" They didn't. Even during our early years when we three slept in the same bed during wintertime to keep warm and I slept in the middle, neither brother touched me. The slightest touch from either, even though accidental, brought a howl from me and rebuke from Dad.

THREE

To Grandmother's House We Go

Child care or baby-sitting, as a profession, was virtually unknown. When parents needed someone with whom to leave their children, they took them to Grandma and Grandpa. So it was that occasionally we three children went to our grandparents' house.

Other relatives and friends were likely to be there, too, visiting Grandma and Grandpa Summers, which made it more fun. I can't remember any visit that wasn't delightful. Grandma heaped our plates with food and we dug in ravenously. That is, after Grandpa returned thanks, during which some of the kids snickered. Grandpa didn't hear them because he was hard of hearing.

Grandma showed us family photos. Some were on cardboard and others were on silver covered plates called daguerreotype. She also had some photos on thin iron plates called ferrotypes. We loved looking at these different kinds of photos.

Grandma had a stereoscope machine which was an instrument that combined the images of two photos to form one of three dimensional depth. We had to look through eye glasses on the machine in order to bring the two photos in focus as one. We loved playing with the machine and marvelled at the images it produced.

Grandma also had a player piano and she let us play rolls of music to our heart's content. We all took turns pumping the pedals to make the rolls go 'round which in turn caused the keys on the piano to play. Everyone gathered around the piano and we sang loudly. Ralph had the prettiest voice.

Grandma let us dance on the dining room table. When my folks heard about this they were displeased to think that she permitted such a thing but they said nothing to her about it.

Mother got along pretty well with her mother-in-law even though they were very different. Whereas Mother was a very clean housekeeper, Grandma paid little attention to disorder. It didn't matter to her that things were stacked up or that the water in the washbasin wasn't dumped as often as it ought to be.

I wasn't disturbed too much by Grandma's housekeeping except when I slept overnight. Her sheets felt like sandpaper. They were made of muslin from flour sacks. I also dumped the washbasin more frequently than it was used to being dumped.

I remember Grandma as being generous. She had some little thing to give each grandchild even though it may be a pencil. Mother said Grandma sold Christmas gifts that she received and that she would take something that belonged to one child and give it to another. According to most of the family Grandma was a wheeler-dealer.

I thought Grandma was pretty wonderful. She seemed to have time for each grandchild even if it was only to give a pat and a compliment. She told interesting stories about the olden days of the nineteenth century and the beginning of the twentieth. She loved to travel and had gone to as many places as she could manage within her tri-state area.

Grandma was restless and active and at any moment might decide that she, her husband and the family should set out for Oklahoma or Arkansas. She would pack trunks with clothing, quilts, cooking utensils and food and off they'd go.

Her tales were exciting about the trips they took in a covered wagon drawn by horses. On one trip they lost their bag of sugar and thereafter everyone in the family drank unsweetened coffee.

Grandma told us about Grandpa's childhood. He was his mother's first child and she died when he was born. His father remarried and had more children.

As a teenager Grandpa worked with his father and half-brothers transporting goods between Independence, Missouri and Colorado Springs. In his late teens, Grandpa "got religion" – the term his family used for conversion. He met Lizzie in the Baptist Church. Grandma bragged that she was the kind of girl he wanted, vivacious and interesting, and so they got married.

After the advent of the automobile, Grandma traveled more than ever. She rounded up anyone willing to tag along and off they'd go in the lizzie, as cars were affectionately called. Grandma's name was Lizzie, too. Elizabeth Ann.

When their children were young, Grandma and Grandpa lived on a farm. Many families lived on farms those days so they could provide enough food for the family as well as adequate housing. Farming didn't require a formal education and land was plentiful. Not many jobs were available for unskilled workers.

My father in 1904.

A farm was a great place to raise children. Plenty of chores kept them busy. They also had horses to ride, small game to shoot and dogs to run with.

Some farms were quite large and others were small acreages. Father and sons worked in the fields, tended cattle, milked cows, chopped wood and did routine tasks. Some built their own houses and barns and put up fences. Neighbors from miles around helped each other, especially in time of sickness or when a house needed to be framed or a barn raised.

During winter the men picked up jobs for cold cash wherever they could. Grandpa chopped down trees, worked in a saw mill and a paper mill and did muleteering.

Women and girls stayed pretty close to home attending needs there and working in the fields when needed.

All the Summers children went to school but it's doubtful any attended more than four years.

Grandpa was a hard worker but when he reached sixty his hands shook so badly from palsy caused by Parkinson's disease that he could work no longer.

Grandpa was reputed as stern. Undoubtedly he had to be, raising all those boys and girls. I remember him taking switches after my brothers. But then, there was nothing unusual about them being in trouble. On the other hand, Grandma was lenient. So lenient, it was rumored, that she undid the good that Grandpa tried to do.

However, Grandpa didn't pay special attention to any of us. What I remember most about him is that he was a praying man.

After Mom and Dad picked us up from visits with our grandparents, invariably Mother would remark about how dirty Grandmother's house was and how stacked up things were.

I remember Mother commenting, "Your mother ought to straighten up that mess and dust the furniture and scrub the floor." Then she added, "It's a wonder that you ever grew up to be so particular, living in a mess like that."

If Dad shrugged his shoulders and said nothing that settled the matter. But at times he would reply, "You've got no right to talk. Look at your relatives. Look at the kind of women your sisters are. And their husbands and kids. They drink too much, don't work steady. And they've been divorced."

An argument would ensue. I remember more than one quarrel about the irreputable qualities of the other one's family.

Mother would answer that at least her family is clean. Dad would make his rebuttal, "So are my sisters. And my brothers."

Word battles usually didn't end quickly but by the next morning normal talk, or lack of any talk, was restored.

Mother's childhood had been very difficult. Her father, Peter Christina, born in Sicily and orphaned as a child, came to America during the latter part of the nineteenth century. He worked as a conductor on a train, where he met a widow traveling with three children. She was French and her name was Abbie Farmer Odena. They married and together they bore three children, the youngest of whom was my mother.

Abbie died in 1907 when my mother was five years old. Abbie was forty-two. Death was due to blood poisoning caused by a miscarriage after Abbie was dragged by a cow. Abbie's death had an especially profound affect upon her youngest child, my mother. Thereafter life for Mother was insecure and tumultuous.

Abbie's three older children were married when she died but the three youngest ones were still at home. Mother's father was

58 years old. He felt helpless taking care of his three orphaned children. Vic, age eleven, left home and foraged on his own as a gardener and a huckster. Mike, age eight, and Rosie, three years younger, went from one half-sister to the other, then to their half-brother or to a boarding place, then back to Papa.

Mike behaved well wherever he went but his little sister, Rosie, found adjustments difficult. She was brokenhearted because of the loss of her mother. Her perfectionistic temperament made it hard for her to get along with anybody. She fussed when anyone touched her belongings. She accused her niece Marie of wearing her dresses, moving her combs and taking her things. She felt rejected and retaliated with rejection.

"We're going to send you back to Papa," her sisters threatened and when she did something that displeased them they took her to her father. He would keep her for a while, but unable to care for her, would send her on the rounds again.

Mother loved ornate and elaborate things. Her photo at age four shows her hands with fingers spread apart so her rings can be seen. Her hair had to be perfect and her garments exact.

A loving family wanted to adopt this child. They took her into their home. They bought her beautiful dresses. One afternoon, however, her sisters stole her away.

Despite the anxiety she caused them, they declared, "No one will ever adopt our sister!"

Mother as a child.

For several months Rosie and Mike stayed in a boarding home where they were treated like servants. While scrubbing pots one day Mike was severely scalded. As soon as their father heard about it, he removed them from that home and kept them for a while. When he heard of a good place to board them he took them there. At this place the man in charge horse-whipped his daughters. When Mike and

Rosie told their Dad about it he quickly took them away from that place and back to his house. Mike set out on his own after that and Mother stayed with a family member until she could work and live by herself.

Mother's desire was that if she ever had a daughter, she would love her, possess her, cling to her. She would lavish on her the things she had missed in childhood. She would make her a model of elegance.

When Mother was eighteen she met Dad and shortly afterwards they married.

Despite a rocky childhood, Mother built strong relationships with her sisters. They were close friends throughout life. Mother visited them as often as possible, taking us children along. Dad said he didn't object "as long as Rosie has my meal on the table on time."

Mother's dreams, however, did not work out the way she hoped they would for a daughter. I preferred simplicity.

FOUR

Kindergarten

Bob entered kindergarten in 1926 when he was five years old. He had to walk a mile to school, uphill on a busy highway. My parents set a firm rule that no child should ever miss school unless he was sick. Bob trudged the road daily with Charlie, the boy next door. Although they were small they struggled through rain, hail and snow.

Three months before I started going to school, my parents decided the road was too dangerous for their daughter and the school was too far away. They decided they should look for a house closer to school.

Jobs had become more plentiful in America and Dad found steady employment with the Terminal Railway Company as a signalman. Steady work meant he was unlikely to be laid off. Also, working for the railroad meant Dad would have a retirement plan. Life had taken a favorable turn.

Dad and Mother found a two bedroom house that they felt they could afford. It was about a half mile from school. They borrowed money from the bank, about eight hundred dollars. The house needed repair and Dad worked hard getting it ready. He even gave up going out Friday and Saturday nights that summer. Dad was shrewd in business and a good carpenter.

In August, 1927 we moved into our new home. It had electricity. It didn't have wall sockets but it did have porcelain light fixtures in the ceilings with sockets in them. We didn't need sockets, however, because we didn't have anything to plug into them. We had an ice box and a wood burning cook stove.

Electric lights were wonderful but their existence brought gloom for us kids and for Mother. "Turn that light off!" she hollered numerous times every day. "You're through with it, aren't you? Don't you know electricity is expensive?"

I'm not sure about how much electricity cost but it may have been close to a dollar a month. Mother was very conservative. She preached thriftiness and harped to us kids that we weren't to waste anything. She would permit some frills but they had to be obtained at a bargain. She tried her best to rub thriftiness on us kids.

Dad earned around a hundred dollars a month. His boss earned twice that much and had an indoor bathroom. We kids considered anyone with an indoor bathroom as rich. Also his boss had a sofa. One of my uncles and his wife had a bathroom and a sofa, too, but they were the ones who didn't have any babies.

Dad built the neatest outhouse in the neighborhood and painted it white. He sawed a little hole for kids and a larger one for adults. Mother tells about the many times she heard us kids screaming in the outhouse. She was sure one must have fallen in. She would run like Jehu only to discover that we were fighting over who would be first to sit on the little hole.

Newspaper torn in pieces was used for toilet paper as well as pages from a catalog. The ink didn't rub off. The paper was a bit stiff but it served its purpose. Manufactured toilet tissue didn't come to our home until the next decade.

When my mother registered me for school in September, 1927 the teacher insisted that my name be spelled M-a-r-j-o-r-i-e not Margie. Mother didn't argue. She had a respect for teachers. Whatever they said had to be true. All documents thereafter have the longer version.

I was the shortest pupil in my class. Dad sometimes told me I was no bigger than a bar of soap after a hard day's laundry. Two of my schoolmates, Frances and Louise, were short also and we became buddies. Being short didn't bother me until years later when everyone grew a lot taller than I.

I remember the day in kindergarten when I told my teacher I had a "heady-ache." What had actually happened was that I had wet my panties. I didn't want anyone to know about it. The teacher undoubtedly suspected my "accident." She told me to go to the cloak room and to sit on the floor. I've always been claustrophobic and I'll never forget the fright I experienced sitting in that foreboding place,

Our parents had nicknames for us children. Mother called Bob "Moses" and somehow associated it with "slow as molasses." She called Ralph "Porky" for pork and beans. Dad called me "Shorty Square" and "Chub."

When Mother considered us old enough to wash dishes that became our task. We three quarreled a lot about whose turn it was to do certain jobs such as washing, scalding, drying or putting them away. All dishes were breakable and more than one fell to the floor and broke. Punishment was unavoidable.

Mother inspected our work and any dish that was not perfectly clean had to be washed again.

Saturday was general housecleaning day. My special assignment was to polish furniture until it sparkled. Mother inspected. When my work didn't please her, which was quite frequent, I'd have to polish the furniture again. My brothers had jobs to do, also, and often they had to redo theirs. They were always eager to go outdoors and play and tried to rush up their work but soon found out, under Mother's careful scrutiny, they couldn't.

A vivid memory of this era concerns bedbugs. They were small insects that parked in bedsteads, especially iron ones such as we had. During the night bedbugs attacked us while we were asleep and left whelps from where they sucked our blood.

Mother was determined to destroy them forever. The only way she knew how to do that was to burn them to death. She rolled up a newspaper and set it afire. Then she held her flaming torch under the bed rails. Bedbugs didn't survive long in our house and I can still visualize her warfare.

Chores done, bedbugs killed and now we had time for entertainment. That meant reading the comic strip in the newspaper. "Little Orphan Annie" had been in print since I was two years old and I sort of grew up with her. Later on Dick Tracy, Buck Rogers, Flash Gordon and Tarzan appeared in the newspaper and in comic books.

In 1928 Dad bought a Victrola phonograph player, powered by a hand-operated crank. We children weren't allowed to put records on it but we were permitted to wind the crank. We listened by hours to the music. Big bands such as Paul Whiteman's became popular and George Gershwin became a famous composer. Songsheets that contained the words of popular songs were published weekly and Mother always bought a songsheet. We sang to our heart's content as we followed the printed pages. Everybody in my family except Dad loved to sing.

In 1930 my brother Bob, who was nine years old, built a crystal set, an early type of radio which didn't have a loudspeaker. The components were very simple. There was a small circuit of wire on a board and a tiny gemlike crystal that made the circuit sensitive to radio waves and turned them into sound. The set required no electricity but it did require batteries. It made a scratchy sound that was barely audible even when we used earphones. I lost interest quickly but Bob and his friends remained excited about it.

Within a year Dad bought our first loudspeaking radio, an Atwater Kent. It had to be plugged into electricity so Dad used the plug in the overhead light fixture. The cord to the radio ran across the ceiling and down the wall. Radio became our new world. We were thrilled to hear distinct, loud speech and music coming from that beautiful piece of furniture. We had a radio before we had an indoor bathroom.

Dick Tracy, Jack Armstrong, Buck Rogers, Flash Gordon and Tarzan still appeared in print but now they dominated electronic sound for us kids. We rushed home from school to listen to our favorite programs. In the evening the entire family gathered around the radio to listen to "One Man's Family," "The Lux Radio Theatre" and other programs. Dad and the boys enjoyed listening to boxing matches. Mother and I never did.

During this era Americans by the thousands were buying their first automobile and many two lane highways were being paved. As early as 1915 the Model T Ford sold well. At that time it was only black in color and had a canvas top. It sold for about $525.

In 1920 the first road signs were posted, such as for railroad crossings, curve warnings and stop signs. A few years after that the first billboards were erected and advertisements were plastered on them. Burma Shave panels on the roadside carried clever messages. Gasoline stations became abundant. The first tourist courts were built.

In 1927 Ford Motors came out with a Model A hard top in a choice of four colors. Of course these new cars cost more money but people loved them.

My cousins, John and Art Phillips, introduced us kids to the Model T. They took us for rides, mainly to show off their vehicle.

The Model T had to be cranked in order to start the motor. A crank handle was located up front near the radiator. While John cranked the motor Art sat in the driver's seat pulling the choke, then pushing the spark handle down and the throttle up. My brother Bob was allowed to help start the Model T when no one else was available. That was a great privilege for him.

A key was used in the ignition. However, my cousins knew how to start a Model T without using a key. They were pretty clever fellows.

Later on John bought a motorcycle and brought it to our house. However, Mother wouldn't let us ride on it.

The first out-of-state trip that my family made was in 1928 but we didn't go by car. Since Dad worked for the railroad he could get free passes on the train for the entire family.

The most outstanding memory I have regarding that trip was not our destination but our getting ready to leave our house. At the last minute some relatives popped in for a visit. They sat around the table chatting until finally it was time for my family to leave. All the relatives got up from the table, pushed their chairs back and left them that way. I went around the table and pushed the chairs under the table where they belonged.

My relatives watched and then they started giggling. What I, a six year old was doing, amused them. It didn't bother me, however. Undaunted, I pushed every chair forward and straightened it. Maintaining order had been so strongly drilled into me by my mother that even at that young age I could not stand to think of chairs being out of place for TWO WEEKS!

Our destination was Boatman, Oklahoma but the closest train depot to Boatman was Tulsa. We traveled those last miles in a jitney, a very small bus. I still remember the narrow roads, chuckholes, crowded seats, fast moving scenery, jolts and bumps. I snuggled close to Dad. That didn't happen very often. Dad knew

I didn't sleep well anywhere except in my own bed and he probably sensed I needed comfort.

We had a great visit on the farm with Dad's sister, Myrtle Gwartney, and her family. Dad had four sisters. All were born before he was and they gave him love and attention as a child, which I believe helped him grow up secure and self-confident. I remember telling Grandma how smart she was to have girls first so they could help her raise all those boys. She agreed.

The trip to Oklahoma was the longest Dad ever took. He disliked traveling but he was patient and uncomplaining during that trip. Mother also, was content.

FIVE

Roses Are Red

At age eight I told everyone that I was going to have ten children. I loved babies. I visited all the neighbors who had babies and gazed at their infants in awe. Several neighbors let me hold their babies. My delight! Those neighbors found me as their frequent visitor. Just ask Mrs. Pasdahl.

When I asked Mother where babies come from she said that the doctor brings them in his satchel. Since doctors made house calls, I kept my eyes peeled for satchels. When I saw a man carrying one I became very excited and asked Mother if he had a baby in it.

My brothers didn't like school but I did. The grocery lady said boys aren't supposed to like school and girls are so I guess that made it alright. I especially liked writing poetry. My brothers did like gym and a few other things. Our parents never helped us with homework.

Mother taught us children ditties which we recited to visitors. We loved to perform. We made wide gestures as we recited:

"Roses on my shoulders, new shoes on my feet,

I'm Daddy's little darling. Don't you think I'm sweet?"

We bowed and our audience clapped. I took to reciting like a duck takes to water, as my Dad would say. I learned early that I need not fear speaking before an audience. Conversation with an individual however, was different. I was scared I might say something wrong.

When Ralph was in second grade a teacher told him "You're dumb." Ralph believed her. He concluded that there was no use trying. He attended school but put forth little effort. He received enough acceptable marks to pass from one grade to the other. Years later, having become an avid reader, Ralph told me, "It wasn't until I was thirty that I discovered I was intelligent enough to learn well."

A major feature of school that we children enjoyed was the moving picture show on Friday afternoons. For five cents we could see a comedy and a feature film in the school auditorium. The feature films were about cowboys, animals and children. The props and locations were simple. Films were made in black and white. We saw "Tom Mix," "Rin Tin Tin," and "Our Gang Comedy." We thought the comedies were very funny. The picture sometimes flickered or halted or sped up. But we were captivated.

Some films came in serial form and a section would be shown each week. Every episode ended with a suspenseful and danger-ous event about to take place, such as a man falling off a bridge or about to be hit by a train. This suspense made us want to return next week to find out how the hero escaped or was rescued. It also provoked agitated discussion all week.

Some kids never had five cents for a movie but my parents made sure their children would not be deprived. Besides, good behavior was bribed toward the reward of seeing a movie.

Movies had been in commercial theatres since before the turn of the century. The first time I went to a commercial theatre was when I was seven. My mother was in the hospital and my cousin Joe took me to the Pantages in downtown Kansas City.

Mother sent us to Sunday School very regularly. The Baptist Church was a few blocks away. My Dad's parents were Baptists so it was logical we should become Baptists. My mother didn't have any church association but she felt that children going to Sunday School, as well as to school, was something all good lit-tle kids did.

Sending us to Sunday School gave Mother the chance to dress us up and thus display her darlings in their best apparel. All three of us rebelled at the stuffy fashions of our flamboyant Mother but she was determined that her children, especially her daughter, not miss the best things in life such as she had missed as a child. A photo of the three of us in new clothes portrays wry expressions.

I liked Sunday School, even the grading system. A new enve-lope was given to each pupil every Sunday on which we scored ourselves. Without fail, and with much pride, I marked myself 100%. Yes, I had arrived on time, brought my Bible, studied my lesson, brought an offering and would stay for the worship service. I also intended to come next Sunday and would invite a visitor (which I seldom did.) It is no wonder I thought you could get to heaven by doing good works!

Every three months we got a new lesson quarterly. I didn't understand all the teacher taught but some of it must have soaked in. We would read verses from the Good Book around the circle. I would count to the verse I would have to read, then study it so that when my turn came I could read it clearly, without faltering.

A hard shell Baptist, they called me. Even a fanatic. Yet somehow, despite whatever happened in my life – misconceptions, failings or successes – I think my heart was tender toward God.

Modern conveniences were becoming plentiful and economical enough for low-middle income families to buy them. These included electrical appliances such as stoves and refrigerators, comfortable living room sofas, bathtubs, toilets and telephones. Lots of families were buying them on time, that is, on credit. My Dad, however, would not buy anything on credit. Except maybe a house if he could find one cheap enough. He said we'd get "fancy furniture" as he termed it, when we could afford it. Which meant paying cash. Even then my parents bought used items.

Dad was a good provider, the term used for a man who supported his family well. However, he loved to gamble and almost every Friday and Saturday night he dressed up handsomely and went out alone.

He'd return home in the wee hours of Saturday or Sunday morning. Mother would be waiting for him and she wasn't a bit timid about yelling at him. Accusations and defenses would fly. Dad was a cool, although guilty, type and he knew Rosie was hot headed. He would try to stave off a fight but it did little good. When we were toddlers we slept through the commotion but as we grew older we'd cover our heads and hide.

Dad ran a gambling table and he did try to remain sober but many times he drank too much and was tipsy when he reached home. Sober or drunk, however, he was in control. After he let

Mother have her say he'd ignore her and go to bed. Mother would scream some choice words and then crawl in bed with me or lay on the sofa.

The next morning she would tell me how mean Dad was and how she hated him. We children sympathized with Mother but we revered Dad.

Several times when Dad had a "bad spell" he got fighting mad. Mother grabbed us children and ran outdoors. We hid behind a barn until Mother dared return to the house. Dad never pursued us. He just went to bed.

The next morning Dad would awaken sick and half repentant. Mother would relate to him how bad he had been. I'd nod my head somewhat in agreement. Dad would reply, "Aw, I didn't do that." The argument usually ended quite abruptly because Mother would threaten to leave Dad and he would walk out of the room.

By mid-morning Dad, sober and serene, would get busy on some chore. Then in the afternoon he'd take the family on a trip, which meant visiting relatives or friends or going shopping. We walked or rode a trolley before Dad owned a car.

I remember only one time when Mother actually left Dad. She took us kids with her to Aunt Emma's house. Dad came after us the next day. He felt sure Mother would be there.

As years went by the occasions of Dad's nights out became less frequent. Alcohol intoxicated him quickly. It made him aggressive, belligerent and daring. Also it gave him nauseous hangovers. At the gambling he became a loser. That diversion which had been so much a part of his life one night came to a halt. But even that did not produce the greatest change in his life that was yet to come.

⁎

SIX

The Great Depression

You must never tell a lie," Mother firmly stated. "And never steal."

"Don't you ever dare let me catch you smoking!" Dad threatened. "And don't ever say bad words." That meant, don't curse.

"If I ever find you drinking, I'll whip you." Dad might be guilty of those things but we'd better not be.

Dad stated axioms with such authority that we knew we must obey. Mother, however, would become very verbal and threatening. Whereas Dad whipped us for disobedience, Mother used additional measures that caused us to be very repentant, at least momentarily. She didn't break our spirits or our wills but she did keep us running scared.

She used policemen as a threat. "If you steal, the police will come after you."

Federal prison in Leavenworth, Kansas also hung heavy over our heads. "If you lie they will take you to Leavenworth," she would say.

"I'm going crazy with you kids," was another threat. "They will carry me off to St. Joe!" The "they" was never identified but we knew that St. Joe was the crazy house. Mother would say, "I'm going to die when I am forty, just like my mother did. You'll be sorry, too. You'll be sorry that you were mean. You'll cry for me. You just don't know how lucky you are to have a mother."

She used non-verbal discipline, too, such as washing our tongues with soap. First, however, she would give us a fair trial. She'd say, "Stick out your tongue." Then she'd say, "I can tell by reading your tongue that you've told a lie." Thus came the soap treatment. She washed our mouth with suds. The procedure was very effective.

Punishment for stealing was having to return whatever we stole. Bob, when he was about nine, stole some candy from a grocery store. Mother promptly marched him to the store and stood at a distance as he returned it to the proprietor. That scared us so much that the temptation to steal was squelched.

Mother made the boys cut slender limbs from a tree and trim them properly. When Bob was about ten, Mother tied his feet and hands with old silk stockings before whipping him so that he could not jump around. Corporal punishment was practiced in many homes during that era. I can still hear my brothers crying, "Forgive me Mama! Forgive me Daddy!"

My parents didn't whip me as hard as they did the boys although I did get my rightful due. While my brothers were being whipped I cried so loudly that my parents felt a few hard stings across my legs was sufficient.

To school we went, at times, with marks on our legs. My brothers were grateful for long overalls and I was grateful for long stockings. Not only did those marks indicate I had been whipped. They also were evidence I had been a naughty girl.

Although Mother gave us spankings she also gave us love. She held us and hugged us a lot. She read us booklets and Uncle Wiggly stories from the newspaper. She told us about things that had happened in her life and she listened to our stories. She sewed dolls and stuffed animals for us. She prayed with us at night.

Seldom do I remember any family members kissing. We just didn't do that in those days. As we grew up Mother told us that her happiest moments were when her babies were tiny and she held them in her arms.

The most fun we had with Mother was when we were away from home. Mother seemed to relax. She enjoyed the adventure of walking through the woods, of picking dandelions and greens, of shopping, of buying hot dogs with chili. She liked to go to the zoo, to the movies or to visit relatives. She enjoyed having them visit us.

The neighbors liked her. To them she was generous, kind and witty. She seldom carried stories about them. She avoided contention with neighbors. Even the untidiness of a neighbor's house didn't seem to disturb her too much.

As a child Mother had longed for approval. She strove to do things perfectly. Her very efforts brought disapproval. Then, as a young adult, her efforts went unappreciated.

Mother attended school only a few years but she had a thirst for learning. She was 29 when I was in third grade. When I arrived home from school each day she asked me to tell her about my lessons. What words were we spelling now? What were we doing in arithmetic? What did we do in language study? I would answer her questions quite simply. But she always wanted to know more.

I told her that the teacher taught us when to use "doesn't" instead of "don't" and to say "isn't" instead of "ain't." You say "iron" instead of "arn" and "can't" instead of "cain't." Not "he done it" but "he did it." Not "tard" but "tired." I have a headache, not a headyache. Mother not only listened. She practiced and changed.

Dad studied, too. Mostly railroad journals. He also read the newspaper thoroughly. Regardless of how "broke" we were, Daddy had the newspaper delivered to our door. However he felt there was no value in sending children to college. Only the children of the rich attended college and that was because their fathers didn't know what else to do with them and had money to throw away.

Dad said he would see us through high school but that was all. Dad wanted us children "to make good grades" but he had no concept of how he could help us or encourage us. He merely expressed pride when we got good marks and disdain for failure.

The summer I was nine Ralph told me that some neighborhood boys had a secret club that met in the shed next door. They invited him to come and to bring me, too. I was glad that my brother and his friends were willing to include me so I walked to that shed with Ralph. Several of the boys were getting undressed. I took one peek, or two, and ran home. Ralph followed me. I was scared but I didn't dare tell my mother about what we had seen. Ralph said that he wasn't going back to that shed anymore and I agreed.

My cousins came to visit us quite frequently. Mother cooked big meals for them and they loved Aunt "Rosie." I especially remember my girl cousin Bertie. She was ten years older than I. I thought she was the most beautiful person on earth. Her blond hair curled just perfectly and she had a quick smile and pleasant disposition. I longed for the day I would be eighteen like Bertie although I knew I could never be that beautiful.

Mother told me several times that she wished I had been a blond. My Dad was blond. Bertie was blond. She wanted a daughter who was blond but she guessed she'd never have one.

When the Great Depression hit America in 1929 my Dad did not lose his job right away. He continued working for more than a year on the railroad. Then one spring day in 1931 his supervisor told him that he was being laid off. However, he said, if Dad wanted to maintain his seniority with the railroad and return to work when things got better, Dad could write a letter once a month to the Railroad Company affirming his desire.

I inherited that job. Every month I wrote a note which Dad signed.

My parents wondered how and where Dad could find work. We had been very fortunate before then to have a steady income. Now, how was he going to be able to support his family? And to pay for our house?

Dad wouldn't accept charity. He worked part time one month for the WPA which was a government program that provided some cash as well as groceries in exchange for labor. Dad hated it. He said the initials stood for We Putter Around and he considered it charity, a blow to his pride.

My uncles had jobs in building construction. Dad worked for them several months. However, for reasons unknown to me he couldn't get along well with his brothers when they worked together. So he quit.

During the summer of 1931 Mother's cousin, Pete Langley, told Dad he wanted to sell a fruit market about a mile east of the house where Ralph and I were born. There was a room at the rear where we could live that winter. Fifty dollars down and two hundred dollars in installments. The price included a pickup truck.

Mother and Dad figured they could "make a go of it." Mom and we kids would help. "Now they are old enough to be of some good," Dad declared.

That summer we left our beloved home and school. A man with a supposedly firm job rented the house but unfortunately within months he lost his job and couldn't pay the rent. Dad didn't have enough money to make the payments and he lost the house to the bank. Thousands of families across America were also losing their homes.

Jobs were scarce. However, a man who did have a job found wages adequate because prices were fairly low but men without jobs experienced great deprivation. Farmers suffered much because their crops brought loss rather than gain. Laborers and young people found employment difficult to obtain.

The Great Depression affected other nations around the world with economic loss. Deprivations that resulted led to social conditions that enabled dictators such as Hitler, Mussolini and Stalin to become powerful.

Despite a failing economy in America new industries, as well as old ones, surged forward in auto making, radio, refrigeration, chemistry and other trades.

Now my parents were the owners of a fruit market on a busy highway. Gas in the filling station next door sold for nine cents a gallon.

It was convenient to have a station there because some people needing gas also stopped at our stand.

My family worked hard. Bob and Dad got up before sunrise several times a week to go to the City Market, They left early so they could get the best buys in fruits and vegetables. Mother helped keep things organized and neat. We had great family togetherness and Dad stopped his drinking and gambling. Well, at least he stopped for some years.

SEVEN

Ice Cold
Watermelon

The first fall and winter in Summers Market, as Dad named his business, went by fast. We lived, rather we survived, in the back room of the market.

When spring came Dad added a small line of groceries to the fruit and vegetables. With Mother in charge of keeping things neat and stocking shelves, our humble store gained customers daily.

"We Aim to Please" was Dad's slogan for the store. He printed ink blotters with the words on it for advertisement. Another slogan was "Honesty is our Policy."

The market was an original drive-in. From the beginning, we gave curb service. Dad also delivered groceries to the homes of customers who would 'phone their orders to us. The market was open from seven in the morning to ten at night. Our family handled the business alone that first winter. In the spring he hired a clerk. We also moved into a rented house on the street behind the market.

Dad decided we needed a lead item that we could sell cheap. He chose milk, in glass bottles, at five cents a quart. Customers came to our market because our milk was cheap and, of course, they bought other items.

Memorial Day was our busiest day. Dad bought loads of pink, red and white peonies at the City Market where he purchased them quite cheaply. Our market was located a few blocks from a cemetery. People stopped by to pick up peonies to decorate the graves of loved ones.

Ice-cold watermelon was our chief drawing card during summer. We wrote the date on every melon so we'd know which ones to sell first. Dad constructed a huge tank into which we placed the melons and covered them with blocks of ice. For a customer to be able to buy a cold melon was a treat since refrigerators were too small to hold melons.

Apples were another good seller. Dad bought them in unsized lots. We sorted them according to size. Then we polished every apple until it glistened. The bigger apples sold for more than the smaller ones.

Mother and Dad were friendly to customers. Mother was especially courteous to salesmen. Her big brown eyes sparkled when she talked with suppliers who brought fresh items daily such as bread, milk and eggs. Frequently Dad was away buying commodities or delivering groceries. Mother mentioned to me how the salesmen complimented her. I know she craved attention and I'm sure she cherished the authority the job gave her.

The school that we children attended was Mt. Washington. The first year was hard for me. When I was in kindergarten through third grade in the other school I had not realized that I was so short and so dark-headed. All the kids in my new school were tall, blond and smart. I stared enviously at Margaret with her long, yellow curls. She was gorgeous, just the way I thought my Mother wished I had been.

My brothers and I were ecstatic about our newly rented house. We had never lived in such a big place. Mother and Dad bought some used furntiure and for the first time we had a living room set, a Kroehler sofa and armchairs. The house had a full size kitchen and an indoor bathroom with tub. It also had a basement, where my brothers installed a shower. We got our spankings down there, too. A nice yard surrounded the house, unfortunately with trees from which switches could be cut.

Mother spent a lot of time in the market so she made me chief housekeeper. I washed clothes in the Maytag washer, hung them on the line, ironed with an electric iron and assumed some responsibility to encourage my brothers to help me. I'm not saying I was their boss. They would deny that although they might say I was bossy.

Dad hired me to cook his breakfast and paid me thirty-five cents every two weeks. I spent every penny carefully. I bought a diary, an autograph book and paper and envelopes for writing letters to cousins and friends. To mail a postcard cost a penny and a stamp for a letter cost two cents.

Two of Dad's brothers worked for Dad for a while. Like everyone else they were trying to eek out a living. Once in a while they dropped in for breakfast so I cooked for them the usual perked coffee, bacon, eggs and toast. Several times I baked biscuits. They always teased me about my cooking. They said my biscuits were duck sinkers or hard tack and called my coffee mud. Of course they always grinned, trying to irk me. Usually I shrugged off their remarks. They, too, might slip me a nickel.

One morning, however, I became so annoyed at their teasing that I took the percolator, full of freshly brewed coffee and dumped pot and all upside down in the sink.

That merely gave my uncles greater cause for delight. Nor did it stop their teasing although thereafter they were more cautious with their remarks. I loved them, anyhow, in my childish way.

Mr. Wilson, the owner of the house we rented, was a well-to-do lawyer. He noted how astute my father was in business. Also that Dad was articulate, neat and self confident. When we had lived in the house about six months Mr. Wilson offered to sponsor my Dad in an education in law. He would promote Dad every way possible, financially and politically.

Dad rejected Mr. Wilson's offer. He would not put himself "under obligation to any man." He would not be in debt to anyone. He considered the offer like taking charity. Furthermore, all his family stood behind his decision. The mentality of the era and his mid-western heritage made the offer unacceptable.

My brothers and I carried the best lunches to school. We each had a sandwich with meat in it, two pieces of fruit and something sweet. Those items put us in a favored bartering position. Some of our schoolmates seldom had sweets or fruit and they would trade us most anything for goodies from our lunch. We might get a marble, a crayon or a slingshot. We even gave away fruit that we didn't want.

I never was a teacher's pet although several teachers gave me attention because of my interest in writing. However, I was an eager volunteer. Sometimes I embarrassed myself by raising my hand so quickly whenever the teacher asked for someone to help with a task.

A disappointment about this new school was that the principal didn't show films on Friday afternoon. Maybe he has a religious conviction against them, I mused. Grandpa did. He even told us that the voices we thought were on the filmstrips weren't really on them at all.

"What you hear is people on the stage talking behind the screen," he said. "And they're making noises back there, too. That's what you hear." No argument could persuade him otherwise. To him it was impossible for anybody to put sound on a wire or on a piece of film.

The new school did have a big play yard and gymnasium. I loved to climb ropes. In baseball I was a good pitcher but a terrible batter. I was usually chosen last when sides were formed. That was embarrassing but the times I was chosen next to last really made me feel good. Somebody out there was wanted less than I was!

I was slow to catch on to jokes. When my cousin told me, "You've got rats in your hair. You need some cheese to catch them," I thought he was serious.

I learned I should laugh even if I didn't catch on. My brothers called me "Dummy" and explained the jokes. Some would just as well have gone unexplained. Even then little kids enjoyed living on the edge of double meanings and colored humor.

Mother spent as much time as possible to teach me to sew, cook and crochet. She was very organized and she encouraged me to be organized. She shared some of the facts of life with me but she did not fill my mind with obscenities. She probably didn't know them anyway. She did let me know that never, in all her life, had she approved of some of the things her sisters did despite her defending them to Dad.

I longed to play the piano. In fourth grade I joined a class that used paper keyboards. However, practicing on paper didn't set well with me so Dad found a good used piano for $25. One of the happiest days in my life was the day that piano arrived at our home.

Mother and Dad undoubtedly had great aspirations for me and they paid fifty cents for lessons with a piano teacher.

However, even with a real keyboard and a private teacher I didn't advance far. I spent hours practicing but I just couldn't play the way other girls did.

Ralph had a beautiful singing voice. A vocal teacher offered him free lessons which he accepted for a while. Bob took lessons at school on the violin.

One of my main diversions during summer vacation was reading love stories from magazines such as True Story and True Romances. Mother and her sisters had quite a magazine exchange. I think they must have bought every issue. Mother let me start reading them the summer before fifth grade. She must have felt I needed some sensorial awareness. I got some early education from those magazines.

That summer, too, it became my job to inspect the elbows and knees of my younger brother to see if, during bathing, he had scrubbed them clean. On one occasion after Ralph did not pass my inspection, I told him, "Hand me the soap."

He retorted, "What do you think I am, your servant?"

I was so disgusted with that remark that I applied the brush vigorously to his elbows. He howled and immediately I was fired from that job forever.

That summer Ralph contracted his first appearance of the Seven Year Itch. His body broke out in a rash. He scratched wherever he hurt and red pustules formed. Mother applied lotion and tried to help him be as comfortable as possible but the rash lasted about two weeks. Thereafter every summer for some seven years the rash appeared again.

In those days kids also got Poison Ivy. Bob and I contracted that intensely miserable rash.

Late that summer I was relieved of some of my household responsibilities. My Uncle Harvey had gotten married and he and his wife, Adele, came to live with us. Uncle Harvey worked for Dad and Adele worked for Mother doing cooking and housekeeping. We loved her. She told us fascinating stories. She played the piano and we all sang. She played games with us and cooked us special treats and German dishes.

I was relieved that Adele took over house duties. However, Adele and Mother found the adjustment difficult.

Adele was not accustomed to trying to maintain a superbly clean environment. Untrained in details considered essential to an extreme perfectionist, Adele found it hard to please Mother. However, she tried. And she learned. Eventually the new bride and the perfectionist somehow came to terms. They survived and even grew to love one another. Undoubtedly because both were made of that tenacious stuff that does not allow one to settle as a loser.

Meanwhile the market business was becoming very profitable despite the fact that some people couldn't pay for their groceries. Dad gave them credit. Most of the debtors paid up but some never did. Dad kept "strict" accounts through the years but never did make charges against those who didn't pay.

Our market was close to railroad tracks on which many trains traveled daily. Men, termed hobos, frequently bummed rides on trains and rode in the boxcars.

As they rode along they would see our market and when the train slowed down sufficiently they'd jump off. They would come to the market and ask for food and money. Mother always gave a man a plateful of food but she would not give him money unless he worked for it. She would hire a man for a couple of hours to cut weeds, chop wood, move boxes or do some outdoor task.

My brothers and I talked to these traveling men. They usually had a destination in mind and a purpose for riding the rails such as going home or looking for a job. They just didn't have the money to pay a regular fare. We found them very affable. Most had interesting stories about places they had been and things they had seen. That whetted our already growing appetites to launch out someday and explore the wide world.

We never met a bum we didn't like! Nor that we were afraid of.

By 1933 Dad had saved enough money, $800, to pay cash for a four door Plymouth Deluxe sedan. Dad tried teaching Mother to drive but they argued too much. Uncle Harvey volunteered to help her. She didn't argue with him and soon she was driving us kids at lightning speed on excursions in the country. She also drove us to town where we visited her relatives.

One benefit that resulted to our family during the Depression was that Dad withdrew from gambling and drinking friends. He had to concentrate whole heartedly upon providing for his family. Also, he had discovered a challenge that absorbed his interest and energy, the fruit market.

EIGHT

The Dust Bowl

"That woman's a fanatic," Mother whispered as one of our neighbors walked out of the store. "She's always trying to get me to go to church and she talks about how good God is."

Mother's comments convinced me that I'd never want to be a fanatic. I liked going to Sunday School but I guessed that as long as I didn't get too religious I'd be O.K.

Mother finally did give in to the woman's invitation and she took Bob and me to a revival. She even walked forward with Bob on one side and me on the other. All of us were crying. I wasn't sure of why we cried but I thought that maybe when you're getting ready for heaven you cry.

After that night Mother didn't go back to church. I continued, however, almost every Sunday. I felt proud about attending church. And I did like it. The Sunday School teacher told us that God would help us control our temper and keep us from bad things.

However, He didn't seem to help me control my anger toward my brothers. We had word battles almost every day and I would tell them off. I wasn't about to admit to them that I could be wrong.

Still, I didn't want to be an angry person. I had seen enough of that in my life.

One day as I was walking to school I thought about how bad my conduct had been toward my brothers that morning. The moment of truth had arrived and instantly I made a decision to curb my temper and my tongue. I prayed that God would help me. I can't say that forever after I found total success but I'll never forget that decision.

A second moment of truth concerned my eating habits. I was one of the fortunate children of The Great Depression who had lots of good food to eat. I piled my plate high and ate every bite. My parents and relatives remarked about what a good girl I was to eat so well and not to waste a thing. They also remarked about how cute my chubbiness was.

I kept getting stomach aches after eating big meals and I began wondering, "Is your tummy supposed to ache after you eat?" I doubted it and decided that maybe it hurt because I ate too much. I made up my mind that I wasn't going to eat so much. I started putting less food on my plate and my tummy stopped aching. Its protrusion shrunk a bit, too.

The world outside our neighborhood seemed small and meant little to me until I was in fifth grade. Geography and history took on new meaning. I learned that there was a big world out there! I longed to see it someday. I learned that Russia had formed the USSR the year of my birth. Communism seemed to make good sense – everybody having plenty and sharing what they had. Members of the press predicted Communism would succeed. That impressed me as did everything I read in newspapers and magazines. By that time I had decided that I wanted to be a writer, maybe for newspapers.

By 1933 Mother and Dad's business had outgrown the fruit market and they looked for a building that would serve as a full-fledged grocery store. They found a good location among a group of other businesses. Above the market on the second story was an apartment which we rented.

So we moved again. I vividly remember those stairs. We children had to scrub them every Saturday. Tenants lived in another apartment on our level but they never scrubbed the stairs. That made no difference to my mother. She could not stand to live in a place with dirty stairs. What would people think?

During the summer of 1933 those stairs did get loaded with dirt. In fact our whole house got thickly covered with dust, inside and out. So were other houses a hundred miles around us as well as streets, land and buildings. No rain had fallen during the summer. The top soil on Kansas farms had turned to dust – ankle deep. Suddenly high winds arose and blew the dust across the miles. It destroyed crops, buried farm houses, obliterated roads and formed dunes. The region struck by this disaster became known as the Dust Bowl.

My brothers and I were outdoors when the wind and dust appeared. I remember being almost blinded by the particles. Dust clogged our noses and mouths and covered our bodies. The noise the wind made was frightening. We had a hard time groping our way to the house.

After the winds died down, Mother described her house as "a filthy mess" and for once, she was totally right. We all dug in with brooms, dustpans, pails of water with soap and rags. It took us several days to clean everything.

Smaller dust storms followed other years but nothing ever compared to the Dust Storm of 1933.

Shortly after that Dad rented space in another shopping area and started his second grocery store.

In September before school started I got my first permanent wave. Short, curly hair was in vogue. Home perms and chemical processing had not yet been introduced. Mother took me to a beauty shop. The operator wrapped my hair tightly on metal rollers. Then she seated me under an apparatus that looked like a large floor lamp with two dozen wires hanging from it. Each wire had a clamp which snapped over a roller. The operator activated an electrical switch and electricity surged through the machine onto the rollers.

Getting a perm was a test of scorching endurance. Seldom did anyone escape a burn on the scalp but during those days nobody sued anybody for such things and we were always delighted to have curls.

In 1935 I graduated from seventh grade. Each of the girls in my class sewed her own graduation dress. To my surprise my teacher chose me to present a reading at the ceremony. "She Sparkled" was the title. Because of Mother's early coaching I didn't find it difficult to speak to an audience. Graduation was a grand occasion. Even Uncle Mike and Aunt Mary came.

During that summer Mother and Dad sold their grocery stores and invested in a "beer joint." My brothers and I weren't allowed to enter the beer joint during business hours but we did go there after-hours. What I liked best about that venture was the shrimp that Mother boiled and served every Friday night as a "come on" for customers. A jazz pianist played my piano which was "borrowed" for the place. On nights other than Fridays Dad offered free pretzels and peanuts to customers.

The joint had several slot machines. Dad would let us drop nickels in them during non-business hours.

Adele and Uncle Harvey helped my parents in the saloon. They needed a baby sitter for their little daughter, Melba, and I had that glorious task. She was delightful. Even though she was barely a year old she could talk well. She could even say "hippopotamus." How I loved to show her off!

Anybody could walk the streets without fear of being assaulted. My brothers and I walked after dark whenever we needed to. At times Melba went with us.

On Friday nights I took Melba for bus rides using a pass which Uncle Harvey bought weekly and that expired at midnight Friday. Melba loved to ride the bus and so did I.

One night, however, the bus driver would not stop for us. Undoubtedly he recognized us as Friday night free loaders.

I went for Uncle Harvey. He came with us to the bus stop and stayed until a bus came. Sure enough the driver stopped and let Melba and me on board.

However, after a month of Friday night rides Uncle Harvey refused to let me use his pass. He said that Melba never wanted to go to sleep on Saturday nights. She wanted to go bus riding first. He said I was "spoiling Melba to death!"

Shortly after that Uncle Harvey and family moved and I lost my baby sitting job.

Walkathons were popular in those days. My brothers and I spent one or two nights each week at one when it was in town. A walkathon was a contest between a dozen or more couples to see who could walk the longest number of hours without passing out.

A large structure similar to a circus tent provided the exhibition area. The platform where contestants walked was in the center. Hundreds of chairs for observers circled it. An orchestra pit and piano were at one side. The music was lively. We loved it. Various artists performed. Walkathon contestants sang as part of the program as well as other vocalists. The contestants always brought the loudest applause. A Master of Ceremonies kept a running commentary using a microphone and loud speakers. My brother remembers Red Skelton as an M.C. He really made things interesting.

Contestants were allowed to rest about 15 minutes every two hours day and night.

The most exciting time came when one partner fell asleep while walking and the other partner had to hold him or her up and try to keep him from falling. If the partner fell, he was expelled and the standing contestant got a new partner. Contests continued until only one couple remained. They became the grand winners. Most contests lasted about six weeks.

Walkathons were outlawed a few years later but while they lasted they were popular. Adele, Mother and we kids had as much fun as being at a circus.

Meanwhile the saloon business wasn't doing too well for my parents. They were investing a lot in it and spending long hours with little gain. Fortunately, at a discouraging time, Dad got his job back on the railroad.

Dad's boss warned him that the railroad company considered a business venture a conflict of interest and if he chose to continue operating the saloon, he would be in jeopardy of losing his job. So he "got rid of the place" by selling it quickly. I was thirteen at the time and was having dizzy spells and strange feelings. Mother warned me that probably what was happening was the approach of a monthly cycle, called the period. Menstrual period, to be exact. She produced white cloths which I would have to wear (and which she would wash for reuse) and she made me a belt. Store bought pads were unknown to us.

I dreaded the coming of that event and it turned out worse than I anticipated. My "visitor" as we termed it, made its debut my first day of junior high.

I felt that everybody could tell that the awful thing had happened to me. Surely they could see the lump on my skirt caused by the cloth under it. And they knew what caused it. I walked stiff legged and felt humiliated.

Mother had wanted everything to be perfect for me that first day. She sewed me a pretty dress, helped curl my hair, paint my fingernails and pluck my eyebrows to a thin line. She encouraged me to be as pretty and relaxed as possible.

She insisted that I wear silk stockings and high heels. Being short, I was rather glad for the high heels even though they were painful to walk in. Some other girls wore high heels, too.

Jeans and shorts were prohibited in classrooms. During gym (now termed phys ed) we wore bloomer-type suits. When we took showers the gym teachers inspected our bodies to make sure we had soaped ourselves sufficiently. We also had to pass finger-nail inspection once a week.

Our high school was twelve miles from our home. Every student had to provide his own transportation. The trolley car and the bus cost five cents for students under twelve and a dime for those thirteen and over.

We tried getting by on five cents as long as possible even when we were too old for that fare. This not only happened on trolley cars and buses but also at theatres, roller rinks, walkathons and wherever fares were required.

Bob and I took a trolley about a mile and then transferred to a bus. We'd drop our coin in the collection box of the trolley and receive a paper, called a transfer, that would permit us to continue our trip on the next route to our home.

It wasn't hard for me to get by with five cents. I was small. However Bob was fourteen and large. One afternoon he dropped a nickel in the money box and asked for a transfer. The driver refused to give it to him. "Put in another nickel and I'll give you a transfer," he said.

Bob didn't have another nickel. Chagrined, we moved to the rear of the trolley and when it arrived at the end of the line we disembarked. Via the transfer I got on the bus but Bob had to walk the rest of the way home, about eleven miles. After that he always dropped a dime in the box.

My first prospective boy friend, Marlin, came along that year. He was sixteen and the brother of my best friend, Lillian Peck. He told me a story of mistreatment that tore at my heart. His girl-friend had broken a date with him and was going to the picture show with another fellow. He asked me if I would take her place. I felt so sorry for him. Of course I would be glad to! At that moment I forgot about a rule my parents had set: "No dating until you are sixteen years old."

Well, anyway, I didn't consider it a date. I was merely help-ing out the brother of my best friend. When I told my parents, however, they reminded me of the rule. They said it would be alright for my younger brother, Ralph, to go with Peck.

When Marlin came to the door he presented me with a flower. I told him quickly that my parents would not permit me to go and added, "But you can take my brother. My parents said it's O.K. for him to go."

Disgusted, Marlin stomped down those clean stairs. Never again was I invited by him to go anyplace! After that whenever any fellow suggested that I go on a date I would tell him about the rule. Although I admired some boys and talked to a few I kept my distance, due to the rule.

After Bob and I had been in junior high four months, my par-ents decided they could no longer afford to pay bus fare and they started looking for a house within walking distance of the school. They found a nice two story rental for twelve dollars and fifty cents a month. It was about a mile from school. So we moved. The house, also, was ten miles closer to Dad's job with the K.C. Terminal Railway.

I had my own room. Mother and I painted it lavender, my favorite color during that time, and she bought me a lavender bedspread and curtains.

Dad and Mother mustered enough money to buy a used din-ing room set and a bedroom set. Very elegant.

The new house had a hot water heater. A gas one. What a lux-ury! It was located in the kitchen. One day my brothers, Mother and I were in the kitchen, our usual gathering place, when I began feeling faint and said, "I feel dizzy."

One of my brothers remarked, "Oh you're always dizzy!" and then I toppled over in a faint.

I sure scared them. They had no idea what was wrong with me. Bob ran across the alley to get help. A neighbor hurried in. "You've got gas fumes in here," he said.

They carried me outdoors. I revived within a few minutes.

No wonder she fainted," the neighbor said. "Carbon monox-ide fumes are coming from that water heater. It's a wonder you haven't all passed out."

He turned the heater off and before we used it again Dad vented it. No more problems.

During vacation the following summer I met fourteen year old Vern at a Salvation Army Camp. We became fast friends. I told him he could not visit me until I was sixteen but we could write to each other. We kept a correspondence going for more than two years. The day I was sixteen he visited me. After a month or so he gave me my first kiss. We learned later that his brother and sister were peeking at us through a window.

NINE

High School and Homemade Quilts

High school was a challenge. Teachers exposed us to new concepts about world affairs and philosophies. I found myself in classes with bright students. Evidently my teachers in grammar school felt I had greater potential than I demonstrated and recommended that I be exposed to students who made good marks.

I was awed by those students yet I didn't feel confident that I could excel. I enjoyed my classes however and my parents accepted my grades without complaint.

My greatest desire was to be a reporter on the high school newspaper. I applied but there was only one position open. Two girls, including me, vied for it. The teacher decided that she would give us a grammar test and the girl who scored the highest would get the position. I scored one point higher than Betty and got to be a cub.

At our first staff meeting I felt like an outsider. All the

High school graduation.

kids on staff had gone to grade school together and they knew each other. Nobody knew me. I determined, however, that I would dig in and prove I could nose out the news. I was on the staff four years and thoroughly enjoyed it.

Our high school had various literary societies proposed to benefit members culturally. In reality, some were snobbish. To belong, a student had to be popular or intelligent or well-to-do. I considered myself none of those. However, some classmates of the same status as I, belonged to the Delta Society, which was considered the most humble. They invited me to join. I did, and that boosted my ego a bit and gave me some clout.

I joined the Pep Club, too, a group of girls who attended basketball and football games and cheered for our team.

I greatly admired smart and talented students. They amazed me in our Latin class, algebra, geometry and shorthand. The students I admired most, however, were the artists. I stood in awe, gazing at their work. Running a close second were musicians. I envied my classmates who played in the band and orchestra and wished I had that kind of talent. I lived from week to week to hear them play during Assembly. I didn't place much value on writers. Anyone could write.

Times were tough in the 1930's. My father earned just enough money to cover necessities. I needed money to pay dues to the various organizations and to purchase a yearbook, a class ring and other items. However, there was no way I could earn money. Jobs just weren't available for teenagers unless you delivered the newspaper, which my brother Bob did for a while. Even baby sitting was done free of charge. I did housework for a piano teacher in exchange for lessons. She always commented about how good I was at housecleaning but she never complimented my piano playing. Anyway she wasn't a very good teacher. She let me play songs that pleased me rather than cracking the whip.

During my senior year my brother Bob left school and joined the CCC (Civilian Conservation Corps) a government sponsored work program for young men who couldn't find jobs. Corpsmen joined for one year and lived away from home in government quarters. They planted trees, drained ditches, did forestry work, tended animals and built reservoirs. They received excellent training and were paid thirty dollars a month plus lodging.

Bob knew I needed money. Every month during his year in the CCC he sent me three dollars from his meager salary to pay for what I wanted. Without him I would not have had them. Rare, dear, unselfish brother.

I enjoyed my friends in high school but I avoided inviting them to my house. I wasn't ashamed of my home, but like some teenagers, I wasn't anxious for my friends to meet my parents, especially my mother. She looked quite Italian and I didn't want to be thought of as Italian.

At that time in Kansas City, Italians, as a nationality, were snubbed by non-Italian. So were Jews, Germans and Negroes. Then one afternoon the inevitable happened.

Mother boarded a bus that I was on. She saw me, walked to where I sat and remarked with tenderness, "Well, hello baby."

I slid low in my seat. An encounter with Mother was bad enough but to have her refer to me as "baby" in front of my schoolmates was humiliating. I didn't return her greeting but looked the other way. She must have realized I was embarrassed, because she walked right past me and sat near the rear of the bus. By the time we reached our destination most of the students had deboarded and I had recovered. I followed Mother out the door and we walked home together. She never mentioned the encounter. Nor did I. Now I wonder how I could have been so obnoxious and she so understanding and forgiving.

Mother did many things, however, that made me proud of her. Crocheting was one and quilt making was another. She was a meticulous worker and every stitch had to be perfect.

Mother was left handed. She hooked her crocheting stitches reverse to the way a right handed person such as I, hooked them. Despite this, however, she taught me how to crochet and we worked well together.

During those days most mothers taught their daughters to do hand work. During vacation time, Mother and I joined relatives and neighbors in quilting bees. A quilt top and its under layers was stretched on a frame made of four wooden slats. We used small needles and thread to stitch a lovely design through the three layers.

Through the years Mother produced fifty beautiful quilts. One is "The Flower Garden." It consists of hundreds of one inch hexagonal blocks spread in a beautiful array.

In June, 1939 I graduated from high school with five hundred other students. The faculty chose me to represent my class as a speaker, not because of high grades but evidently because they thought I presented an acceptable speech.

College was out of the question for me. My parents didn't approve. Dad said college was only for sons and daughters of rich people. They didn't really go to college to learn. They went to pass time away and to associate with other upper class young people.

At sixteen I faced the working world. I had to find a job. Any job. I applied at one place after another. Jobs were scarce and hundreds of teenagers were out looking.

I was small. Nobody wanted to hire me. Catalog houses needed husky helpers. Business places wanted people who had experience or were better qualified.

After about a month, I got a job in a cafe serving tables. Within two weeks the business folded. Several weeks later I got a job as a biscuit server in an elite restaurant which specialized in having short girls carry buns, hot from the oven to diners. Two of us girls carried buns. We wore Dutch costumes. The waitresses wore white uniforms. The pay was low but it was a job. Social Security had begun and I obtained my card.

Eight waitresses worked in the restaurant. Before business hours we met in a large dressing room to put on our uniforms. Listening to their conversations I learned a lot about worldly affairs. One of the waitresses bragged about having an affair with a customer and started sharing details. Another waitress whispered to me, "Don't listen to her. It's not worth hearing. She's not up to any good."

Before long the other bun girl and I became chummy and soon we were going places together after hours. We went to dances at a nearby ballroom. I met a couple fellows there who asked me for a date. None tugged at my heart strings but I did accept invitations just for the fun of it. However, my Dad found something wrong with every fellow who came to our house to pick me up. He was either too old or too young or he didn't have a good job or he came from the wrong side of town.

I felt Dad had good judgment but I also speculated that I never would find a fellow who pleased him. Fathers those days bragged that it was unlikely any man would ever be good enough for their daughters. Dad told me several times, "You'll probably fly over a blossom and land on a manure pile."

My brother Bob brought friends around and so did my girlfriends but I wasn't satisfied with any of them. My family said I had my share of boy friends but I know differently. Many evenings I felt rejected and lonely. I was the proverbial unfulfilled maiden.

Through one of my friends I met a young man who immediately met Dad's disapproval. He was twenty-one, had been married and was divorced. Dad warned me that if I continued dating him, he would make me quit my job at the restaurant. That was the worst punishment that Dad could mete out because without work I would be without wages.

The next evening Dad spied on me as I was leaving my job. He saw me getting into the fellow's car. He walked up to me and ordered me to come with him. I obeyed quickly. Dad was a person you wouldn't dare disobey.

Dad drove me home reiterating the facts that no one in his family had ever been divorced and none of his kids would ever marry a divorced person or get a divorce. Maybe Rosie's family got divorces but his never did.

The scene that followed at home was not a pleasant one. I defied Dad with what he termed "sassy talk." I rebelled at his telling me what I could and could not do. During the argument Dad hit me. I ran to my room crying.

I never went with that fellow again although he did try to contact me. Dad made me stay in the house for a week. The word "grounded" wasn't popular usage but that is what happened to me. Meanwhile I lost my job.

Alone, with time to think, I made a decision that affected the rest of my life.

❧

TEN

The Candy Concession

I found myself without work again and with little potential for obtaining a job. I didn't want to be a waitress but I had no other experience. I thought about being a reporter but despite several interviews no newspaper had a spot for me.

I considered secretarial training. Several of my friends were taking secretarial courses. One recommended that I contact the junior college. There wasn't any charge for classes there. I visited the registrar. She said that the secretarial course lasted two years.

Two years! That was a lifetime! I wanted a quick education and a quick job. Anyhow, I doubted that my parents would support me for two years while I went to school. The registrar suggested that I contact a business college. Their courses didn't last so long.

I inquired at several business schools. Their courses took from eight months to a year but all of them charged fees plus a down payment. That left me out.

I read an ad in the Kansas City Star stating that a business college was looking for a girl to work in their candy concession in exchange for tuition.

I called for an appointment with the president of the college and after an interview he accepted me for the job. The semester of typing and shorthand which I had in high school gave me a head start. The course also included bookkeeping.

A co-worker of my father drove me to class every day as he went to work. He wouldn't accept any pay for my fare. He said he was pleased to do my Dad a favor.

The candy concession was located in the lobby of the college. I sold quite a lot of candy but when business was slow I did my homework. It was an ideal setup.

A fellow named Bill stopped by almost daily to buy a chocolate. He chatted and joked. Many of his sentences began with "Confucius says" and finished with some original proverb. I thought Bill was quite clever.

One of my assignments was to read "How to Win Friends and Influence People" by Dale Carnegie. I internalized every sentence. I wanted to be the kind of person the author advocated.

Seldom had I expended great effort in my studies but now I did. Typing lessons required that I type ten perfect pages of every lesson with no erasures. Speed was not pressed beyond reason. Accuracy was stressed. This was one of the best disciplines I ever received. Shorthand was difficult but I passed the tests. Bookkeeping was easy. I was surprised that I could do so well. It took me eight months to finish the course.

At the graduation ceremony there were four graduates. The college president told us that the first thing we should do was to take a Civil Service exam. The United States Civil Service, he said, paid higher salaries than any other business. "Although," he added, "if you are accepted you may have to move to Washington, D.C. Most clerical positions are available there."

I was prepared, so I thought, to get a high paying job immediately. I asked Dad about working for Civil Service. He stated emphatically that I could not go to Washington. Yes, I could take the test but I could accept a job only in Kansas City.

Civil Service jobs were becoming quite available due to the escalation of war in Europe. Within a week a Civil Service exam was given for typists and I was one of the fifty persons who competed. Typewriters were not provided and each of us brought our own. I was never more nervous in my life. My final score showed it. I got a passing grade but it was below what I had hoped. I felt certain Civil Service would never hire me, especially since I said I wouldn't work anyplace other than in Kansas City.

A week later Montgomery Ward hired me as a typist in their corporate office which was about a mile from my home. I made twenty-eight cents an hour and worked forty hours a week.

Having a job was great but after several months I began feeling dissatisfied. I felt unfulfilled and wondered if anything or anyone would ever fill the emptiness.

Mary Akers, my neighbor and high school chum, told me that she had found a fellowship that was the best thing that ever happened to her. She went to a place called Central Bible Hall. She wanted me to go with her.

I was bored with my present church going. The way she talked about hers intrigued me.

One Sunday I went with her. I was delighted to find that Bill was there. He was the fellow who had visited the candy concession.

The Bible had been taught to me like a story book and I never really thought of internalizing its teachings with life changing results. Here, however, they specialized in that. The Bible, as Mary had said, was taught in an interesting way and was made applicable to everyday life. As well as life everlasting. The Sunday School teacher, Anna Mae, was beautiful but she said you had to accept Jesus as your Savior and be born again. Well, I had gone to church all my life. Wasn't that enough?

Anna Mae read the Bible to us girls, Ephesians chapter two "For by grace you are saved through faith. It is the gift of God, not of works lest anyone should boast."

I always thought that trying to do the best you could will get you to Heaven. I knew there were things that I had done that weren't exactly right but I thought that maybe God would forgive me anyhow. Nevertheless I felt an emptiness that longed for fulfillment.

Anna Mae explained that a person cannot gain heaven by just trying to do good, but must receive Jesus as Savior. That worried me. One night I knelt by my bed and told God that if Jesus wasn't in my life I wanted Him to come in right now. I wanted to be forgiven of my sins. With simple faith I believed. And I received a peace that has never left.

Thereafter I began to devour Bible study and the more I studied the more convinced I became of its life changing power.

My attitude toward Mother changed. I respected her in a new way and no longer felt humiliated by her nationality.

Mother was not happy when she heard about my conversion. She said, "You'll never have any fun now. You ought to be out dancing. The only time you have fun is before you get married." Little would she believe that I was having the best time ever.

Dad, however, was pleased. His father was religious and his sisters were religious. His Mom even attended the Salvation Army. Dad may have thought he could stop worrying that I might get pregnant out of wedlock. Church girls just didn't do that, he seemed to think. At least his sisters hadn't done it.

The young people's group had a meeting at my house one Saturday night.. Mother seldom allowed any of her children to bring friends to our house because she couldn't stand anyone "messing it up." This time she not only consented but she baked a cake and she dressed elegantly for the occasion.

However, by the time the young people were due to arrive Mother had worked herself into such an insecure state that she began feeling ill. She went upstairs to my bedroom, disrobed, put on a nightgown and went to bed. I begged her to dress and to come downstairs but she became very angry. She accused me of preferring Mary and those other people to her.

Several of the young ladies had looked forward to meeting my mother. I told them she was not feeling well and had gone to bed.

"May we visit her for a minute?" one asked. To visit ill people was a common practice of this group.

"No," I replied. "She really doesn't feel like seeing anybody." It was a humiliating experience for me but I was afraid for them to talk to her lest she say something I wouldn't want my friends to hear, such as how I was wasting my life spending time with them.

The evening was delightful anyway. A gifted pianist played my piano and we sang songs and choruses. Then we played a game or two and had a brief Bible study and prayer followed by refreshments. That evening the treasurer of the group, Al, paid me special attention. He asked me if he could pick me up the next morning and take me to church. We dated about six months.

When Al met my father, Dad asked him, "Are you bonded as treasurer for the money you collect from your group?"

"No," Al replied. "God is my bond." That made a great impression upon Dad. He couldn't believe that anyone who collected other people's money would go unbonded.

The next day Dad asked me, "What do you think that young man meant when he said God is his bond?"

"That his faith in God holds him morally responsible," I answered. "He has to be honest because he would have to answer to God if any of the funds were missing." Dad marveled at the concept.

On my job at Wards it didn't look promising that I'd have a salary increase for a long time or a more responsible position. Still, I was glad to have a job. To my surprise, after two months my salary was raised to thirty-two cents an hour.

A fringe benefit of working at Wards was that employees got a ten per cent discount on purchases. Mother loved the privilege. She and I benefitted from the discount.

Our store was the headquarters for mail order outlets throughout the midwest. The bargain basement was filled with returned, rejected and surplus items. Mother always had an eye for bargains and our great delight was to shop at Wards. She bought some of the fineries of life which otherwise she would not have possessed.

I paid five dollars weekly for room and board and Mother invested it in purchases at Wards.

The possibility of America entering war hung heavy over us those days. Great Britain and Germany were in the throes of World War II. Government and political leaders of the United States vowed our country would not become involved. Franklin D. Roosevelt was our President.

Then came the sneak attack on Pearl Harbor by the Japanese on December 7, 1941, a day none of my generation will forget. The American naval base at Hawaii was bombed. Thousands of American servicemen were killed and many battleships were destroyed.

The United States was plunged headlong into war. Immediately there was an escalation of new factories for the production of armament needed for battle. The induction of civilians into the armed forces began. Women started working in factories that produced implements of war. Three shifts of employees worked around the clock. Thus the term "swing shift" was created.

Everybody, it seemed, was getting a job in a defense plant. Warren Bailey, who had been my brother's buddy in the CCC told me that the defense plants were paying fabulous salaries. He had just got a job at Remington Arms in Lake City, a nearby suburb. He was sure I could get a high paying job there, too. All I would have to do was to take a Civil Service exam and apply. I was not so sure. I had already taken an exam and had not done so well.

To my surprise a telegram was delivered to me at home. Telegrams provided the fastest way to send printed messages. A telegram meant important business! This was the first one I had received. Tearing it open I read that I was offered a clerk typist position in Washington, D.C. with the Federal Government. There was no other choice of location, the telegram stated.

Dad figured that the reason the job was available was because the parents of decent girls would not allow their daughters to go to Washington. Neither would he consent for his daughter to work in that corrupt capitol.

"Any girl who is worth her salt wouldn't live in Washington!" Dad stated.

I was nineteen years old. According to Dad he was responsible for me until I was twenty-one. I wondered if he would feel that way about me for the rest of my life but I didn't dare ask. In his opinion daughters should always live at home except in very unusual circumstances such as to teach school in the country, perhaps. I would have gone to Washington had I been permitted. I speculated I'd never have another opportunity and I might be working for Wards the rest of my life.

Meanwhile I became more involved in activities at Central Bible Hall. Young people from various Christian colleges presented programs. They sang beautifully and were good speakers. I thought, "How wonderful it would be to go to a college like the ones they go to: Wheaton, Bob Jones, Biola."

Ten young people of our group attended college somewhere away from Kansas City. They joined our activities during summer but were gone during winter except for the Christmas holidays. I looked up to them. I revered them. I envied them. I mused that if I got a job earning lots of money I would save it and go to college.

I remembered that Warren Bailey told me that Remington Arms in Lake City needed clerk typists and was offering fantastic salaries. I also reminded myself that my Civil Service score wasn't too good and it wasn't likely they would hire me.

"Well, I do have some work experience now," I told myself. "That might help."

My newfound trust in God came to mind. I thought, "If God wants me to attend college he can help me get a job in a defense plant. I'll promise him that if I get a job earning a good salary, I'll save every penny that I can and I'll go to a college next fall where they study the Bible." I prayed about it and made my promise to God.

To myself I mused, "But I don't want to go to a school in Kansas City. I want to go someplace like Illinois or Tennessee or California."

I prayed, "Dear God, You'll have to do a great work in my Dad's heart. He'll never let me go anywhere unless he gets convinced."

I didn't feel I was making a business deal to God. I was making Him a promise. I prayed with faith believing that if God wanted me to go to Bible College He would work miracles. And He did!

ELEVEN

World War Two

"You have to take a Civil Service exam," the receptionist said. I was in the downtown office of Remington Arms on a Saturday morning applying for a typist job at the munitions plant.

"I've already taken a Civil Service exam," I replied.

"Well, we have to give you another one," she said. "The only scores we accept are from tests taken here. Would you like for me to schedule you?"

"Yes," I replied, then asked, "Should I bring my typewriter?"

"No," she answered. "We supply everything."

That was a relief.

A week later when I returned for the test, three girls were also there to be tested. One was a friend from Business College. Immediately I relaxed. I was glad not to have too much competition.

The following Wednesday I received a telephone call from the clerk. My score was acceptable and a job was available. The pay would be one hundred forty four dollars a month.

I felt like shouting, "That's a fortune! I'll earn more than a dollar an hour."

However I merely replied, "Yes, I'll be glad to accept the job." Then I added, "But I have to give two week's notice at my present place of employment."

"That's fine," she replied. "I'll schedule you to report at the Lake City plant in two weeks."

The days that followed were filled with excitement and anticipation. My supervisor asked me how much I would earn. When I told her she was surprised.

Word got around quickly and soon fellow workers were asking me if it was true. Suddenly I, a mere junior typist, had status.

Wards paid a fair wage for that era but the defense industry, vying for workers and secured by government backing, enticed prospects with salaries that could not be equaled by secular businesses.

To reach Lake City I rode a bus for an hour. However, Warren Bailey had told me that if I got a job I could join a car pool and the driver would pick me up at my home.

The result of my physical exam was acceptable. An escort led me past several large one-story buildings to another huge one. Inside this building was the Requisition Office where I would work. I typed requisitions for supplies needed at the plant. I had to type five copies of every requisition, without error if possible and then proofread them. After making corrections, if needed, I passed my work to another girl for proofreading. Five other typists in my pool did the same type of work.

I had never typed on an electric typewriter but for the next eight months typing was my major assignment.

Warren had told me I'd find a ride in a carpool within a few days and I did. Because of a wartime shortage of gasoline, gas was rationed. Coupons for buying gas had to be obtained from a rationing station. Employees who transported other employees got extra coupons. I was in a carpool with three men who were kind to me but when I caused them to be delayed several times the driver warned me, "You either get ready on time or you look for someone else to pick you up." I got ready on time!

The oldest worker in my office was twenty-seven. She was our supervisor and she seemed quite old to us young girls. Most of us typists were in our late teens.

However, Wilma was a typist and she was twenty-two. She became my best friend. Her mother had died while Wilma was in high school and Wilma had the responsibility of helping raise three sisters. I visited them in their home. Wilma and I shopped on Saturday afternoons and she went to church with me several times.

Wilma had a steady boyfriend, a nice guy named Lee Marstellar. They decided to get married. They set the date and place for their wedding. Wilma asked me to stand with her as a good friend. I felt honored and bought a new dress. It was made of a newly-manufactured synthetic material.

Wilma wanted to reserve a room at a hotel in Excelsior Springs for their honeymoon and she asked me if I knew anything about making hotel reservations.

"Not really," I replied. "But I'll be glad to help you if I can."

"Well," she said. "I was just wondering if I should ask for a room with a single bed or one with a double bed."

I pondered, then answered, "I'm sure you'll want a single bed. You don't want to spend your honeymoon in two different beds."

Wilma telephoned the hotel and asked for a room with a single bed as I had suggested.

The wedding took place at the home of Wilma's aunt. I had to take a bus to get there and rain poured down in torrents as I scurried to her Aunt's house. My dress got soaking wet and the synthetic material curled upwards until it barely covered my thighs. As the skirt shrank it puckered. When I arrived at the house, Wilma's aunt answered the door. I told her what had happened and asked her for a large towel to wrap around me. She brought one and we rushed upstairs. Fortunately the stairs were near the front door and I didn't have to greet anyone.

My predicament caused a delay in the ceremony. Wilma's aunt produced an iron and ironing board. I took the dress off and we ironed it, pulling as hard as we could to smooth it and lengthen it. Finally the dress was in an acceptable condition and I joined the wedding although I stood at the back of the room. I was embarrassed.

However, an event just as vexing happened to the newlyweds when they arrived at the hotel.

I'm sure they were glistening with nuptial joy when they requested the room that Wilma had reserved.

The clerk looked puzzled. He asked, "Are you sure you want a room with a single bed?"

"Well, we just got married," Lee stated. Undoubtedly he spoke rather quietly.

"But that room has only one narrow bed," the clerk replied.

The clerk studied the bewildered pair for a moment then turned aside and consulted another employee. After a few minutes he returned to the honeymooners and said, "Our honeymoon suite isn't occupied tonight and we've decided to let you have it for the price of the single room, if you like. It comes with flowers, champagne, breakfast..."

I imagine the newlyweds sparkled as they looked at one another and shook their heads.

"Oh thank you! Yes, we'd love to have the Honeymoon Suite," Wilma told the clerk.

Elegance galore. Innocence rewarded.

When Wilma returned to work she was radiant as she told me about my error and the result. Lee, however, never gave up teasing me.

In January, 1942 I took part in another wedding. My best friend, Mary Akers, married C. R. Johnson. He was six feet four inches tall. His brother, six feet six, was best man. Mary asked me to be her bridesmaid. I knew that the wedding party would seem strange with little me standing next to those tall fellows so I wrote a note to Mary. I appreciated the honor but I didn't want to spoil her wedding. I suggested that Mary's sister stand with her. Mary then asked me if I would light the candles. I was delighted and the wedding was beautiful.

During those months in 1942 I experienced some very special friendships. I was having fun yet I didn't forget my promise to God about going to college to major in Bible studies.

I wrote to various colleges for information and application forms. I corresponded with friends who were students. What was their college like? How much was the tuition? What did room and board cost?

One of my friends, Agnes Bollin, attended Biola in California. The name of the college stood for Bible Institute of Los Angeles. Agnes wrote me encouraging letters. She loved the teachers and the classes. There was no tuition although there was a small fee for registration. The cost for room and board was reasonable. The dormitories were in the tallest building in Los Angeles, thirteen stories high. By early summer I decided that Biola was the college I wanted to attend. I made application and was accepted.

In late July I told my parents that I was going to quit my job within a month and go to school in California. You would have thought I set off a bomb! I had told them earlier about my plans but they didn't think I was serious.

"You'd give up a good paying job for something like that!" Dad exclaimed.

"Yes I would," I replied. "God provided that job so I could save money to go to Bible College."

Dad retaliated, "You saved money because we provided a home for you! I think God would have you appreciate that!"

"I do appreciate it!" I exclaimed. Then I added, "I'm hoping you'll get a pass for me on the train to Los Angeles. You said you can get them for me until I'm twenty-one."

Dad was angry. "If you think I'd get you a pass on the train so you can go free without paying to California, you have another thought coming."

I retaliated, "Then I'll pay my own way."

Two strong wills were at battle! I turned and walked away.

The weeks that followed weren't easy. My brothers had been inducted in the Army and were transferred to other states. Mother grieved that her sons had gone to war and now her only daughter was planning on leaving her. She told me many times how foolish I was to give up a high paying job. She reminded me that I only paid five dollars a week to live at home and here I was gadding off to some unknown place without money or job.

I avoided confronting my parents. I knew there was an element of truth in Mother's accusations but I didn't want to hear them.

The week before I left my job Dad called me to talk with him on the front porch. I felt certain he wanted to make a final appeal for me not to leave.

He asked, "Are you still determined to go to California?"

"Yes," I replied.

"Nothing is going to stop you?"

"Nothing."

"Then, how would you like for me to get you a pass on the train?"

I was surprised. "I'd like that very much," I answered. At that time, I did not realize the total significance of his concession. I thought he was merely helping me save money. In reality he was expressing love, confidence and relinquishment of control.

Dad seldom demonstrated affection. How could I interpret his helping me as being anything other than monetary? Now I realize there were dozens of ways he showed love and I did not recognize them. Nor did I recognize the love of my Mother. Hers was possessive love, yet it was there.

The Summers family, 1940. Grandma and Grandpa are seated with their four daughters. Bob and Ralph are at the corners. Margie is fourth person from the left, top row. Mother is second person to Margie's left and Dad is next to boy in hat. The others are family members.

TWELVE

Venture West

Mother drove me to the railroad station. At last I was on my way to California. Soldiers filled the depot and they were the first to board the train and to get seats. Mother was fearful about my traveling and especially during war time. No one in our family had ever taken such a long trip.

When I boarded the train not one seat was vacant and the aisles were already crowded with people who were standing.

My having to stand added to Mother's fears. "Are you sure you want to go?" she asked.

"Yes, I'm sure," I answered. "I'll be alright. I'll sit on my suitcase." I promptly showed her how I could do that. Several passengers who were standing moved aside and shrugged their shoulders as though they thought I was presumptuous but I didn't care. I had to appease my Mother's fears.

"You could wait for another train that isn't so crowded," she suggested. She probably visualized me sitting on my suitcase all the way to California.

"No, Mother, I'm not waiting. I'll be OK," I had heard that there was no such thing as a train leaving Kansas City that wasn't crowded.

"You know that since you're riding on a pass you won't be able to take a seat as long as a soldier or a paying passenger is standing."

"I know, Mother, but I'll get a seat pretty soon. Don't worry."

Mother stayed until the last call for visitors to disembark. We hugged. Tears smarted her eyes as she left.

I waved to her as the train pulled out of the station.

The ride was jerky and about as slow as a tortoise. We stopped frequently for passengers to detrain and embark.

Fortunately more people detrained than boarded. Paying passengers and servicemen filled vacant seats quickly. The conductor walked down the aisle checking tickets.

My suitcases were directly in front of an exit door. Whenever the train stopped, I'd jump off for a few minutes. I was curious. I guess I wanted to see what every station looked like. We hit a lot of rural stations in Kansas.

I sat on my suitcase five hours before I got a seat. Fortunately, I got one next to a window. Soldiers got off and on the train at various stations. I initiated conversations. "Where are you going?" I asked. After he answered I told him where I was going and what I'd be doing.

I rather enjoyed the trip. I felt relaxed, unhurried, no pressures, no exertion. At night I covered my face with my coat and slept as best I could. Being short of stature was an asset. I could nestle quite comfortably in my seat.

During the day I wrote poems about the scenery, the trip, my adventure and my faith. At times I shared my poem with whoever was sitting next to me. Passengers even seemed interested. I was helping them kill time as we crossed barren plains.

The trip took three days and two nights to reach Los Angeles. Biola was located in the heart of downtown Los Angeles and was in the tallest building in the city. My dorm room was on the thirteenth floor.

The elevator which took me there looked like a bird cage. Cables that held it could be seen in the open shaft. A trained operator ran the elevator. He was needed because the elevator was prone to miss floors by ten inches or more when it stopped. The operator had to ease the cage slowly into a position level enough for passengers to disembark.

Into room 1354 I carried my luggage. Agnes was there to welcome me.

New students were invited to take a bus tour of the city. Already I was enthralled with Los Angeles and wanted to see as much as I could.

The bus driver greeted us before we started and asked us to introduce ourselves. "Also, tell us where you are from," he said.

Betty was from Oregon, Ruth was from Texas, others were from other states. I was from Kansas City.

"Kansas?"

"No. Missouri."

"How many of you are from the South?" our driver asked.

Several raised their hands. The guide asked them to tell where in the South they were from. "Texas." "Louisiana." "Mississippi."

"Southern California! And my name is Art," shouted one young man. Several students laughed. I looked at the fellow. He was grinning from ear to ear.

The tour was interesting. I got acquainted with several new students.

When we registered for classes, most of the subjects were already assigned to us. However, I was able to enroll for piano lessons. My practice room was on the basement level.

Arthur also enrolled for private lessons although he was studying voice. His practice room was next to mine.

I could hear him trying to peck out notes so he could vocalize. He had a hard time finding the right keys. He could also hear me practicing. One day he came to my room and asked if I would help him for a few minutes with a lesson.

I consented. After that I helped him two or three times a week despite the fact that the college had a rule that students were not to practice in the same room. I rationalized that it was alright for me to help Art by playing the notes he should sing. He had to prepare for a weekly radio program on which he sang solos.

Art had a good voice but I considered him a bit eccentric. He tried to make jokes about everything. He was very outgoing.

He worked swing shift in a defense plant and attended classes during the morning. He roomed with a blind student named Earl. His mother lived thirteen miles from Biola in El Monte and Art drove home on weekends.

It seemed that even outside class Art and I frequently encountered each other. Several hundred students attended classes but Art was the one who'd be in the lobby whenever I happened to be there, or in the library or in the dining room. Those encounters plus our practice times meant we saw each other, or at least passed by one another quite frequently. Usually we'd say "Hi" in passing. Art was five years older than I which I, at twenty, thought a bit old.

Another student, a quiet one named Don gained my attention. He was in his second year at Biola and he invited me to attend the fall banquet. I reminded him that a school rule stated that first semester students could not date. He said we wouldn't be dating. He would merely buy me a ticket and we'd meet at the banquet.

Don bought two tickets and signed my name next to his. The Dean of Women called me to her office. "You know that first semester students are not permitted to date," she said.

"Yes, I know."

"Then why did Don sign your name next to his?"

I explained what had happened. She replied, "Well, you can go to the banquet but you can't sit together. When next spring comes you can, if you like."

I told Don what the Dean of Women had said and that I didn't want to get in trouble. I asked him to please invite a girl who wasn't a first semester student.

I felt certain he would do as I requested. However, he didn't.

On the evening of the banquet Don sent a corsage to my room. He hadn't given up! That really upset me. I asked Agnes to telephone him to meet her in the lobby. She could tell him I wasn't well and then hand him the corsage. By that time, it was quite true that I felt ill. Agnes did as I requested. After that I avoided Don as much as possible.

Agnes was an inspiring roommate. She motivated me to study hard. I had always admired students who made high marks and Agnes made A's. She told me that if I studied I could also make A's.

Agnes guarded her quiet time and refused to idle away any moment. She worked fifteen hours a week to help pay her room and board. Her life illustrated discipline, efficiency, purpose and love.

During second semester when dating was permitted for freshmen, Art asked me to go to dinner with him. We went to Clifton's Cafeteria. Clifton's was an elaborate restaurant decorated with jungle decor including many plants and flowers. Performers sang from a platform high above a pool while an organist played a pipe organ.

Art had a car. He was one of the few students who did. On our second date we visited his mother in El Monte. Other times we drove to the beach and to Forest Lawn. We double dated several times with his friends, Ross and Wanda.

Every student had a Christian service assignment. Mine was to teach a Sunday School class of nine year old girls. Art took me and the girls to a park with a playground.

Art brought me a corsage almost every Friday night and at times he handed me a box of See's chocolates. I enjoyed his generosity but I was merely having fun, thinking little about romantic involvement.

I had ideas about what I thought a prospective husband should be like and although Art was very kind to me, he didn't seem to fit the mold. Maybe I had been influenced by too many romance magazines when I was a girl.

Still, he did have qualities I admired. He was talented. He was kind, a fact demonstrated by his willingness to room with a blind student named Earl. He had time for everybody. When he encountered fellow students he shook hands. I'd notice them grinning at times. I thought it a bit strange, too.

Art was a good student. He made excellent grades. That impressed me. I was uncertain, however, that I wanted him to be more than a friend. It was convenient to have a boyfriend who cared, yet I felt uneasy about it. At times I treated him coolly but he never seemed to notice it. His lack of criticism of me made me admire him. Meanwhile his family became aware that something had smitten Art, their bachelor brother.

During that semester at Biola, through lectures and studies I felt God was calling me to be a missionary. I wondered how Art would react to that. Agnes had a special love for the people of South America. I thought perhaps God was calling me there, too.

When I told Art he said that he, too, had thought about mission service, perhaps in missionary radio. Electronics was his favorite avocation. Recently he had heard the wife of the founder of a radio station in Ecuador tell about the work there. It made him wonder if somehow he might be used in radio to reach people with the gospel. However, his mother was dependent upon him for financial support and he wasn't too sure.

I was interested in radio, too. I worked part time as secretary for a broadcaster and typed commercials for a radio agency.

Art and I took walks in downtown Los Angeles several times just for recreation. That great city was practicing blackouts because our country was engaged in World War II. Many buildings were barely lit up. Most lights were extinguished during nighttime. Windows were covered with black shades to help obscure buildings. Every precaution possible was taken to hide the big city.

The basements of buildings and the passages of subways were converted into bomb shelters in case of an enemy raid. They were eerie places. One spring evening Art and I decided to walk into a bomb shelter to see what it was like and it was there that he asked me to marry him.

I wasn't too startled but neither was I too certain that I wanted to get engaged. I reminded him that I had decided to become a missionary and I wouldn't want to marry anyone who did not feel the same as I did. He assured me he did.

"What about your mother?" I asked.

"She will get along OK," he said.

He seemed nervous. Suddenly he remarked, "There is something I have to tell you."

I wondered, "What can it be?" He was so nervous that I wondered if he had been married before and hadn't told me.

He stated, "I have a terrible temper."

I smiled and thought, Is that all? I replied, "I have a temper, too. I guess everybody has a temper."

"Well, my mother said I have to tell you."

"Your mother?" I questioned. The only time I had seen him quarrelsome with her was the Saturday she asked him to repair a chicken coop. She said that he had promised for weeks to repair it and some of her chickens were getting out.

He had turned on her in anger, "You always have jobs for me to do when I come home! Why don't you leave me alone?"

I sympathized with Art. I was impressed, also, when later that day he repaired the coop although he muttered to himself while doing it.

Art now said, "I might be drafted for military service."

I argued, "But you are working in a defense plant and you're attending Biola. You can get deferred on both counts." I cringed at the thought that he would even consider sidestepping his schooling to go into the Army unless he had to. That certainly would delay his becoming a missionary.

"I'm tired of having my neighbors gossip that I'm a draft dodger," he said.

"I wouldn't care what the neighbors say," I told him. "What is right for you is right and is no concern of theirs."

Immediately he changed the subject. Never had we discussed anything pertaining to sex but suddenly he said, "I want you to promise that when we get married you will never have an abortion."

I smiled. It was just like Art to bring up a new subject when he wanted to evade the present one! "Of course I will never have an abortion," I agreed. Topic terminated. I accepted his proposal. We were engaged with little idea of when we might be married.

Financially, Art's earnings were good but expenses related to school, auto payments and providing for his mother kept him strapped.

However, I was not aware of his financial situation except that he always seemed to have plenty of money for whatever he wanted.

We decided to go shopping for rings. We found a lovely set but the jeweler would not let Art take it until he paid for it. Art put down a few dollars to hold it. He tried to get a loan but the bank wouldn't give it to him because he was of draft age. Although I didn't know it at the time, Art sold the motors to his model airplanes to help pay for my rings.

Still he didn't have enough money. The banker said he would loan money to Art if he transferred the title of his car into his mother's name so he did and got the loan. He proudly brought the rings to me. I had no idea of the measure to which he had gone to pay for them.

Six years before I met Art, he and his mother had bought a half acre of land in El Monte. They borrowed money to build a house. Art was nineteen and he did a lot of construction on the house: wiring, plumbing, brick laying and carpentry. When he proposed to me I had only a little knowledge of the very gifted fellow he was and I had no concept of how seriously plagued he was by a volatile temper.

He had many hobbies. Not only did he pursue electronics and model airplanes he also liked to paint, enjoyed photography, loved to sing, tinkered with automobile repair and read voraciously. He was a self described "absolute perfectionist." His meticulous ability at detail made him a careful worker but it also made him difficult to work with because he was hard to please.

Art was not gifted in letter writing but I insisted that he write to my parents asking for my hand. It may have been one of the toughest assignment he ever had. With my prodding, however, he wrote the letter in his very finest penmanship and mailed it. My parents were duly impressed. I had already told them by mail what a fine man he was.

I returned home to Kansas City when the school year ended in June. I proudly displayed my engagement ring.

I got my old job back at Remington Arms during vacation. Mother and Dad even consented for me to live at home without paying board.

The previous September, Mother had turned her life over to Christ. She told me that she had been very lonely and had nowhere to turn except to the Lord. She remembered things I and others had said about becoming a Christian. She prayed. Now she no longer felt alone and felt secure. Her attitude was affected. Mine was, too.

THIRTEEN

Soldier-Boy Husband

The husband of my best Kansas City friend, Mary, was inducted in the Air Force and sent to North Africa. Mary was lonely without him and she decided to go to California with me when I returned for my second year. She, too, would attend Biola. In September, 1943 we traveled together and she became my roommate.

Second year studies were interesting and beneficial. However, I found that getting my homework done was difficult because I had to work long hours at part time jobs to meet expenses.

In early October, Art told me that he had been reclassified 1-A. I pleaded with him to try to get a deferment. He could qualify on two counts: defense work and ministerial student. However he refused. He felt some loyalty to enter the conflict but mostly he disliked the criticism of neighbors who were calling him a draft dodger.

My heart was set on us continuing our studies until graduation. I hoped he wouldn't pass the physical. He had very flat feet, which supposedly was a hindrance on long marches and might disqualify an inductee. However, in October, 1943 flat feet were no determent. Art may not have told the examiners about them. He passed with flying colors.

Three weeks later he reported at Fort MacArthur, the induction center. That day, November 6, 1943, was one of the gloomiest in my life. I hated to see him go and figured he might be gone for years. He was assigned to the Army Corps of Engineers. After spending ten days in California he was sent to Camp Abbot in eastern Oregon for basic training.

Art wrote me a letter every day. Postage was free for servicemen. All he had to do was print the word FREE in the upper right corner of the envelope.

The pressures of school and work became more stressful daily for me. I had not earned enough money during the summer to carry me over. Emotionally I could not handle bills going unpaid and was surprised that some students didn't feel the same way that I did. I realized that the professors needed money and that if we students didn't pay our bills they wouldn't get it. Furthermore we had some of the best Bible teachers in the county of Los Angeles and their salaries were low.

I also strove to make high marks which put me under added pressure. As the end of the semester approached, I began feeling dizzy and faint. My work and study schedule was too heavy. I knew I could not continue and pondered taking a break. I wondered, should I return to Kansas City for a semester and a summer? I felt certain I could get my old job back.

I wrote Art about my problem and he answered, "Let's get married." He said we could finish our training together when the war was over. He also said he was lonely. He would like for me to be near him. If I were his wife he could get an allotment from the Army for my support. It might not be enough to live on but I could get a job on base and that would help. He was certain my experience with Civil Service would put me in good stead for finding employment. Also, he would give me what extra he could manage from his salary.

His suggestions sounded like the best option. I much preferred going to him than going to Kansas City. By correspondence we set our wedding date for February 2, 1944.

One of my friends at Biola told me she had friends in Bend, Oregon, the closest town to Camp Abbot. She contacted them. They would meet me at the bus station and help me find a place to live. Her friends turned out to be the wife of the pastor of the Nazarene Church and her sister. They did everything they could to help me.

Art had experienced some unfortunate illnesses during the two months he had spent at Camp Abbot. A few days after he arrived he was hospitalized with influenza. After two weeks he returned to his Company. Within a few days his temperature soared and he was diagnosed as having scarlet fever. He spent another two weeks in the infirmary, after which he was returned to his training cadre. However, some glands swelled on his neck shortly thereafter and he was diagnosed as having mumps. He spent two weeks in the mumps ward feeling fine. No wonder he had time to write me a letter every day! Released again, the glands on his neck began to swell, his temperature soared and be became very ill. The earlier diagnosis of mumps was mistaken. Because he had spent two weeks in the mumps ward he had contracted them. Back to the infirmary he went, extremely ill. He had just been released a few days before I arrived.

Each time Art was sent to the infirmary the unit with which he was being trained had to be quarantined three days. Recruits could not leave their barracks. Art's hospitalizations set back four companies in their schedules. Also, it took him twice as long to finish basic training as it should have.

Art was feeling fine when I arrived but he couldn't get liberty to leave camp the first weekend so we postponed our marriage to Sunday, February 6.

The Pastor's wife suggested that we have the wedding in the church after the morning service. I liked the idea of a congregation in attendance.

The ceremony was simple. I wore a white dress and hat that Mary had made for me and carried a corsage of hybrid Irises. I had hoped for an orchid but the nearest town where one was available was Portland so I accepted a substitute. Art was handsome in his army uniform.

One of Art's buddies stood as best man and the daughter of the minister was my bridesmaid. Two ladies sang, "Like a

February 6, 1944

Shepherd Lead Us" and "The Lord's Prayer." Art was so nervous he trembled. I couldn't keep from smiling.

We knelt for prayer. Art's knees made a creaking sound as he knelt. He looked at me and grinned, then frowned. For me the marriage ceremony was an adventure. For Art, I think it may have been a frightening experience.

The minister's wife had baked a cake and decorated it with a soldier and bride. She invited the congregation to a reception in the parsonage. Someone took photos. A dozen people brought us congratulation cards but there were no gifts. We expected none and were grateful for the gifts of love bestowed upon us.

Art and I walked to a studio where we had photos made and then we ate lunch in a small restaurant. Art had asked his staff sergeant for liberty that Sunday night but the sergeant informed him he better be back on base by three in the afternoon or he would be AWOL (absent without leave) which, during war time, meant court martial.

We spent our honeymoon miles apart. I was in a cold, one room shack in Bend and Art was in his barracks at Camp Abbot.

The next day I started looking for a job.

Bend, Oregon was not a prosperous job market. After walking around town and making inquiries, without any encouragement, I went to the local employment office. I filled out an application form, gave it to the secretary and sat there the rest of the afternoon, hoping someone would call saying they needed a secretary.

The next day I took a bus to Camp Abbot and was informed that the only place where they hired civilian employees was in town. So back to the employment office I went and for three days, hour after hour, I sat in the office hoping to be called.

My strategy worked. On the fourth day the secretary in the employment office didn't show up. The office manager asked me to substitute for her. The secretary was absent two weeks and I worked in her place.

The office manager, realizing how desperate I was for a job and how earnestly I worked, telephoned an official at Camp Abbot and asked him if he could use me. The official said he needed some secretarial help and I should come for an interview. I got the job! No one on earth was happier than Art and I! We heartily thanked God for His provision. It meant I could stay!

The following weekend Art's sergeant softened and granted him a two day pass. Thereafter Art was able to come home weekends.

During our second weekend together on a Saturday afternoon we went to the home of two of the ladies who had been so kind to us. They had discovered how well Art could sing and they wanted him to practice with them for a trio which they would present in church.

The ladies complimented Art about how beautiful his voice was and said they appreciated his singing with them.

I was proud of Art but I did a foolish thing. I noticed some shaving cream in one of his ears. I touched his ear and said, "There's a bit of shaving cream here. Let me rub it for you."

Immediately he turned on me in anger. "Don't you ever tell me what's wrong with me! You understand?" he firmly stated.

I backed away, shaking my head affirmatively. The ladies seemed startled momentarily but when Art turned toward them they resumed their practicing.

I was embarrassed. I lowered my head and waited. By the time the trio had finished singing I had recovered somewhat from the shock of his rebuke. As we walked home, we were silent. Fortunately the weather was cold and it didn't matter that we didn't talk.

As soon as we arrived home Art started "setting me straight," as he called it. He said that he had put up with a lot from me during our courtship. He had taken it then but he wasn't going to take it any longer. He said I had treated him unkindly many times. I had ignored him and he had let me get by. But no longer would he stand for it. Never again was I to criticize him. He had a God given right to be respected and obeyed.

"Do you understand?" he asked.

I nodded affirmatively. Tears were stinging my eyes but I held them back.

Art grew angry because I didn't talk. He said I was stubborn and sulky. He said I was always nice to everybody else but I wasn't always nice to him and he wasn't going to put up with it.

I knew I was guilty, at least partially. There had been times when I had avoided him. Times when I wanted to be with my girl friends rather than be with him. But he had always treated me lovingly and acted as though I never offended him.

I explained that I hadn't meant to criticize when I mentioned the shaving cream. I just wanted to help him. He ignored my explanation.

I said, "I'm sorry." Then he said he was sorry and we became lovers again.

Similar confrontations occurred on other occasions. In fact, they occurred quite frequently. Art made quick accusations and always silenced my rebuttle. "Don't you hold a grudge," he'd say.

I had never been a quick forgetter. But then, neither had I been so quickly accused. I preferred thinking about things before debating them. Art called that "pouting" and he said he hated it.

I began wondering, "Apparently he disapproved of my behavior before we married. Why did he marry me?" I also wondered why I had married him.

The Monday after our spat, when Art was in camp and I was alone, I faced a decision. Did I want to spend the rest of my life with him? I could have the marriage annulled. I could take a bus back to California or to Kansas City. What should I do? During those moments I made a firm resolve, a commitment. I would stay with Art the rest of my life. I would go where he would go. I would try as best I could to please him and to cooperate with him. I recognized his excelling qualities. I would love him for the good person he was.

I didn't tell Art that I had faced the crossroad and had made a decision.

Although Art was very critical at times, at other times he showed consideration. There was the time I burned the fried potatoes and he merely remarked, "I like them that way."

Our encounters were an eye opener to me concerning myself. They made me realize I was a proud person. No one had crossed me or accused me the way Art did. My mother was reputed as crabby but she never charged into me so fiercely.

Relatives said I was "the apple" of my Dad's eye. He bragged so much about us kids that it seemed to them that he thought we could do no wrong. In Art's eyes I wondered if I could do any right!

Art and I discussed our feelings. He was very sensitive about his self-assessment and I had to be cautious and non-accusative. Many times I pardoned his anger as not being his fault. In many ways I don't think it was. He had inherited weaknesses as well as strengths. His mother's family had a history of mental maladjustment.

Art refused counselling. During those days many people, both Christian and non-Christian placed a blight upon it. Art stated that if you had things right with God you didn't need counselling from man, especially from professional counsellors.

When he was a child his father made him say he was sorry for everything he did that was out-of-line. To say "I'm sorry" became a habit. As an adult Art apologized for reaching for the salt, for walking across the room and for a dozen non-offending motions. Seldom, however, did he seem to recognize when he injured a heart.

Art always had an extreme bent toward perfectionism. As a child, when things didn't go right, as they frequently didn't, he blamed the nearest person for whatever went wrong. Often the nearest person was his sister Viola. Their non-English speaking, jovial Norwegian grandparents took the boy's side and defended him.

Some of his accusations were so ridiculous that the family laughed at him. Then he would throw a tantrum, lay on the floor, kick and scream. His mother scolded, his sister teased and Grandma pampered. On one occasion Art threw such a fearful tantrum that the neighbors called the police to investigate.

In kindergarten Art had difficulty adjusting. His behavior was erratic and he had attention deficit. His teacher required him to repeat his kindergarten year. When he was in eighth grade one of his teachers discovered Art's unique abilities in electricity and shop and gave him special attention and encouragement.

As Art passed from his teenage years to his twenties he began to realize how seriously his temper controlled him rather then he controlling it. He felt sad and guilty about it and yet proud. In many ways he was satisfied with the person he was and yet he was very dissatisfied. He concluded that he was the way God created him and wished that in some ways, especially when it concerned his quick temper, that he could be different.

Art attended church quite regularly with his Mother. He felt that church attendance might help him resolve some of his problems. He participated in Sunday School and was elected secretary of his class when he was nineteen.

One Sunday the minister preached that everybody is a sinner and needs to be saved from everlasting loss to everlasting life. He said that an uncontrollable temper is unpleasing to God and that God can give power to curb it. Art felt convicted. He admitted to himself that he had some problems and he needed help.

When an invitation was given for people to walk to the front of the church, Art walked forward. Some of the people were surprised to see the Sunday School secretary come forward but he acknowledged his need and pled with God for forgiveness.

A change did come about in his life. He became more tender and more understanding of the needs of others. His fowl language disappeared although his perfectionism didn't.

Being a Christian became a way of life for Art and a source of power. The more he learned about the teachings of Christ and the Bible, the more he wanted to learn. He talked with his pastor who recommended that Art attend Biola and it was there that we met.

 za

The Newlyweds

Our marriage went quite smoothly once I got straightened as to what to expect and how to adjust to whatever might occur. Also, Art was becoming adjusted to me.

His mother visited us that spring. I enjoyed being with her and she seemed to approve of me. However, she and Art encountered problems and they debated them openly. She had sold his car and deposited the money in the bank in her name. She said she sold it because gas was rationed and cars were selling for high prices. She told me that Art had consented to the sale. Art denied it.

His mother had her displeasure, too. Art had transferred his army insurance from her name to mine. If he was killed in action, I would get the entire insurance. That distressed her because she was dependent upon him for support.

Art was displeased because his mother had deeded 160 acres of homestead property to his brother. It was supposed to be divided among the three children. His mother said she did it because she couldn't pay the taxes and she knew Art couldn't. Nor his sister.

Somehow the problems were resolved and after that we had good times together. When she left for California she seemed happy to have visited us. We were happy that she had come.

Art and I lived in Bend five months after which he was transferred to Ordnance School in Tacoma, Washington. His mother gave us the money she had deposited from the sale of his car and we bought another one, a 1937 Nash coupe.

Art spent four months in Tacoma and then was transferred to Camp Claiborne, Louisiana. We drove there by way of California where we visited his Mother and family and then to Kansas City where we visited mine.

While we were in Kansas City Dad was building a garage and Art helped him for a week or ten days. Dad admired Art's willingness and his ability to do various jobs.

At Camp Claiborne I was hired as a clerk typist and we lived on base. A letter came from Art's best friend, Alvin Wright, that he had become the father of a baby boy. That gave Art the urge become a father.

He told me, "After all I am 27 years old. I don't want to be too old when we start having children."

However, I didn't want to be a mother. Not yet. I wanted to wait until the war was over and Art was out of the Engineer Corps.

Art won the debate and soon I was pregnant. And very nauseated. I continued at my office job until I was six months pregnant and would have continued longer but Art received orders that he was being transferred to Fort Belvoir, West Virginia.

We decided that I should go home to Kansas City and live with my parents until the baby was born. My parents graciously consented.

Those months in Kansas City before the baby arrived were happy for me – relaxed, fulfilled, anticipating. I was glad to be with family and friends. I didn't realize until then how much I missed them. Mother was very kind and never fussed at me. Dad was considerate although rather quiet.

Mother had started attending church regularly. Dad went with her at times. They seemed happier and more content than I had ever known them to be.

My pregnancy was not problematic until time came for delivery. Suddenly I developed a uremic condition in which toxemia caused my body to swell as well as my hands, feet and face. My blood pressure, which normally was low, was very high. When the doctor ordered me to the hospital, my feet and hands were so swollen that I had to wear my Dad's shoes and remove my wedding rings. I objected to the latter, saying, "People will think I'm not married."

Shortly after arriving at the hospital I went into eclampsia, a convulsive state, and had eight convulsions within two or three days.

Mother and Dad were frantic. They spent many hours at my bedside. I was not expected to live. My parents wired Art and asked him to come to Kansas City as soon as possible.

Friends at church prayed for me and the baby. Several visited me but my face and body were so swollen they hardly recognized me.

The doctor gave me medication to induce labor but the medicine worsened my condition and the baby would not drop into position. He consulted with several others doctors. They decided he should not operate lest I convulse during surgery and die.

For nourishment I was fed intravenously. I was given injections of morphine. That caused me to hallucinate. I saw little, pregnant women and soldiers on the ceiling.

Penicillin had recently been discovered and was successful in the treatment of wounded servicemen. My doctor ordered the nurses to give me a penicillin injection every three hours. Dad said they thought I was a pin cushion.

For five days I remained semi-conscious yet alive. On the fifth evening a nurse told my parents, "She is going to die soon unless they operate." Yet the doctors did not operate. They hoped I would suddenly improve and deliver normally. Also they feared that surgery might kill me.

My parents stayed at the hospital until ten-thirty one night. When they arrived home they had scarcely set foot in the door when the telephone rang.

"You daughter is dying," the nurse said. "Return to the hospital at once if you want to see her alive."

They returned, exhausted, and spent the entire night with me and yet I did not die. Friends and family prayed. God spared my life.

The next morning the doctors decided they must operate or both the baby and I would die that day. The baby was showing signs of distress. Its heartbeat was irregular.

I was prepped for a Caesarean section and wheeled into the operating room. The doctors had decided I could not have anesthesia lest it kill me immediately. A surgeon wiped the surface of my abdomen with a pain deadening solution and made the incision. I felt nothing.

Once the baby was removed, I started recovering. The baby was fine. Thank God! A pediatrician examined our new little daughter. She was healthy and beautiful. Weighing six pounds two ounces, she was born on September 7, 1945. We named her Janice Diane.

I needed a blood transfusion. Blood flowed directly from the veins of my father into my veins. That was how transfusions were given those days.

My parents had suffered much. Art arrived several hours after Janice was born. Paper work had delayed his coming but he was grateful to be with us. While flying in the airplane, he had sensed God speaking to him, assuring him that I was alright and so was the baby. It was with great confidence and joy that he entered my room.

❦

FIFTEEN

War and Postwar

I was dismissed from the hospital three days before Art was scheduled to leave for Fort Belvoir. I was weak from surgery so Art took care of the baby during the night. He changed her diaper every hour and by morning he had used a dozen diapers. We had no clean ones left. Disposable diapers were virtually unheard of and the only clothes dryer was the line outdoors. Mother quickly laundered diapers and hung them out to dry.

Art was supposed to attend to the baby's needs the second night but he was so worn out that not even the baby's cries could awaken him. The care of the baby became my task with my husband supervising.

I was too ill to breastfeed the baby so Art bought bottles, nipples and canned milk to which we added water and syrup for the formula.

"The nipples have to boil five minutes to make sure they are sterile," Art announced.

Nipples were made of rubber and when they boiled the holes in them swelled shut. The baby sucked on the nipple but no milk flowed from it and she cried. Art heated a needle and poked holes in the nipple. The holes were quite large and milk gushed out when the baby nursed, causing her to choke.

Art bought new nipples and boiled them for five minutes. The same thing happened again.

I telephoned the doctor. "We think there is something wrong with the nipples that we buy," I said. "The milk comes out too fast and the baby chokes."

"That's strange," the doctor replied. "None of my other patients have complained about them. Maybe you got a bad batch. Try a different brand."

Art bought another brand of nipples. They, too, swelled shut after boiling and had to have holes poked in them. The baby gurgled and choked but somehow she survived.

After Art left for his army base nipple problems ceased. Mother and I didn't boil the nipples.

Janice and I stayed at with my parents until she was two months old. Art was anxious for us to come to Virginia, where he was stationed, and I was anxious to be with him. Now that he was an instructor in an engineering cadre he could live off base with his family.

Our next home was in Arlington near Washington, D.C. On weekends we took excursions to our capitol city. We visited the Smithsonian Institute and the Lincoln Memorial.

World War II ended and in March, 1946 Art was discharged. On our way to California we stopped in Kansas City. Arriving in California we stayed with his mother a few weeks and decided to rebuild the double garage into a small house. We borrowed $700. and bought the materials we needed. Items such as windows were not yet available and Art built the ones we needed.

I worked alongside Art every day. I learned a lot about building construction. Years later Art and I built other houses and I enjoyed the work despite my exacting boss.

Art did everything from drawing plans to moving in. He laid foundations, did framing, plumbing, electrical work, cabinetry, finish work and painting. In addition to working alongside him I was bookkeeper, purchaser, go-fer girl and cleaner-upper.

Our monetary income was very small. Jobs were scarce and California was flooded with ex-G.I's. Art reported weekly at the employment office and was never offered a job. We spent several months refurbishing the garage so we could live in it. Art also picked up jobs repairing radios and doing house repair.

September, 1946 rolled around. We were ready to enroll in Biola. Art qualified for schooling under the G.I. Bill which provided tuition plus a small living allowance.

Art attended classes five days a week and I attended three days. My mother-in-law took care of Janice while I was in classes. She became very attached to the baby, who looked a lot like

Janice in 1946.

her. At the time I didn't realize how attached a grandparent can become to a grandchild.

Biola was thirteen miles from our home. Gasoline was about twenty or twenty-one cents a gallon. A fellow student provided transportation for us most of the time in exchange for services that Art did for him.

During the next two years our lives were filled with studies, work, family and church. We graduated from Biola in June, 1948 with diplomas in Biblical studies.

Art was very strict with Janice. He would tell friends and relatives, "She is the only child we'll ever have and we've got to make sure she's not spoiled."

He eyed her constantly concerning her behavior and slapped her hands for the slightest offense such as reaching for something on a table or playing with a pillow. He reprimanded her continually with "No, no." In many ways, also, he manifested his love for her. He held her, hugged her and told her he loved her. He expressed pride in her.

Fortunately Janice was a compliant and happy child.

Art frequently remarked that if he had been handled properly as a child he would not have the problems he had with his temperament. He didn't want Janice to have the same problems.

Neither did he want me to have another baby because of the near death experiences I had during the delivery of our daughter.

I felt, however, that we needed a second child. Art's attention would be divided between two. I became pregnant. Lovely little Gloria, weighing eight and a half pounds, was born on January 23, 1949.

Our family had outgrown the renovated garage. We decided to borrow more money and build a second home. Despite having two children to take care of, I helped Art just as much as before. He hated to work alone.

We had not forgotten our desire to be missionaries. The thought was continually in our minds. Art wanted to work with Christian radio overseas but he felt he needed more training in the electronics field. He was entitled to more schooling under the G.I. Bill and thought about attending a technical school.

His friend, Ross Wright, suggested that he go to John Brown University in Arkansas. Ross said that Art could earn a degree in engineering which would provide prestige in the electronics field. His credits from Biola would transfer. The G.I. bill would provide tuition and books and we could rent an apartment on campus.

Art applied and was accepted. The converted garage rented for $35. a month and the new house rented for $65. Financially we felt secure.

September, 1949 found us traveling to JBU with our two daughters. Janice was four and Gloria was eight months old. Art drove our 1936 Plymouth pulling a box trailer loaded with our possessions.

We had almost reached JBU when we ran out of gas. We had spent all our money except five cents. We sat contemplating what to do when a young man riding a bicycle stopped and asked if we had a problem.

"We've run out of gas," Art said. "We're on our way to John Brown University."

"Oh, I work at John Brown," the young man replied. "I'll be glad to buy you some gas and bring it to you." He left saying, "I'll be back in a few minutes."

True to his word he returned with a can containing thirty-five cents worth of gas. I wrote down his name and telephone number and promised to pay him as soon as we could, which I did.

Art and I were grateful for the provisions which awaited us at JBU. Our apartment had three rooms plus a bathroom. It was located on the third floor of a dormitory building that had been converted into apartments for married students. Those living there were mostly ex-G.I.s.

The apartment didn't have much furniture but Art and I found a table and chairs that we could borrow and an icebox and other items. We had brought our washing machine and beds in the trailer. The rent was $22. per month which included gas, electricity and heat. We felt it was a provision from the Lord.

Students could buy groceries on credit at the commissary and we did.

Staff and teachers opened their hearts with expressions of love. The administration allowed ex-servicemen to postpone all expenses including tuition and books until their checks from the government arrived.

During our first two months our car remained unmoved in the parking lot. It needed some minor repairs as well as gas but we didn't have the money for either. My grandmother, who lived eighty-five miles from the University, died four weeks after we arrived and we couldn't afford to fix the car to go to her funeral.

The week of Thanksgiving arrived. We would have four days of vacation from classes. My parents wanted us to drive to Kansas City to spend the holiday with the family. With a bleeding heart I told her we couldn't go and I explained why. Within a few days a check came from Mother for twenty-five dollars, enough to make the needed repairs and the trip. What a celebration we had that weekend! My parents were delighted to see Janice as well as their newest granddaughter, Gloria.

Three months after we arrived at JBU our first check from the government arrived. It included all back pay. I'll never forget that day. We held the check up, waved it, looked at it, laughed and cried. Then we ran to cash it and pay all our debts.

JBU permitted the wives of veterans to take some courses without charge and I enrolled. During our five semesters, I earned thirty credits.

All students at JBU were required to have a work assignment outside the classroom. During our first year Art fulfilled his by preaching in a small country church in the town of Summers, Arkansas. The congregation couldn't afford to pay a salary but every Sunday they invited us to dinner and loaded our car with vegetables from their fields. We loved the time spent with those folks.

During his second year Art became a shop teacher. He was honored with an engraved medallion, the highest award given to a student teacher.

During his senior year Art designed and constructed the first television receiver ever to be on campus. He used parts that he had brought from California plus some he bought at surplus stores and from friends. His TV was quite a novelty to the engineering students who came to our apartment to see it. Programs were received by transmission from Tulsa, Oklahoma.

I didn't watch very often because the picture flickered and the sound was quite static. However, the engineering students seemed to enjoy it. They asked Art questions about its components and conversed in engineering verbiage that I didn't understand. Anyway I was too busy with children, cooking, school, church and missions activities to watch fuzzy TV such as it was those days.

Four months before Art graduated we wrote a letter to Radio Station HCJB in Ecuador, South America to ask about applying to serve there. Office personnel sent us application forms which we filled out and returned. Within a month we received a letter saying that the Board of Directors would be meeting in Chicago and they would like for us to go there for a personal interview. We said we would be happy to meet with the Board.

Taking a few days off from classes we drove to Chicago, stopping overnight, of course, in Kansas City. While in Chicago we visited Art's grandfather, who died several months later.

We arrived at the stated time and place with our two daughters for the interview. Two hours passed. I was fearful that the children might act up but fortunately they didn't. Finally the Board Members were able to talk with us. The interview was brief and we headed for JBU, wondering if we would be accepted.

Years later, Dr. C.W. Jones, the president and founder of HCJB, told me how favorably impressed he had been at that time with our children as well as with my "multi-talented" husband.

Joining the mission meant we would have to raise pledges for our monthly support. The mission did not pay anyone a salary.

Optimistically we felt our church friends and others would stand behind us. In fact we felt we would reach our quota by mid-summer but a surprise was in store for us.

SIXTEEN

Mission Support

Art graduated from JBU in May, 1951. Our next step was to get pledged support. We headed for California via Kansas City. When we arrived at my parents' home we found that a devastating flood had hit the Kaw and Missouri Rivers in northeast Kansas and northwest Missouri. Many companies were in need of qualified workers who could help repair damage done to electronics facilities.

Art offered his services to Trans World Airlines and was hired for the emergency. He was sent to various towns to repair damage that had been done to electronics equipment.

The children and I went wherever Art went, usually to small towns in Kansas. We always found rooms to rent and stayed two weeks or longer in each town. Art drove our 1936 Plymouth pulling the box trailer. Many roads were barely traversable because of flood damage. We got stuck several times but someone always came along to help us. We unpacked the trailer at least five times and set up housekeeping. We didn't have beds so we slept on mattresses on the floor. The job lasted three months which was longer than we had anticipated. Art was paid well and we were glad to have the money.

TWA asked Art to remain as an employee but we knew that if he accepted we would be deterred, perhaps permanently, from our mission.

When we finally arrived in California one of our houses was available so we moved in. We thrust headlong into deputation work seeking support from friends, churches and anyone else who would be willing to pledge funds for our family to serve in Ecuador.

Our first visit was to the pastor of the church where we were members. He was new to the congregation and to us. Within minutes we discovered that he had firm feelings about supporting mission organizations that were not sponsored by his denomination. He would not back us. Disillusioned, we left his office. We felt that some of our friends in the church might support us but we chose not to present our ministry to them lest it cause contention.

First try: struck out at home base. But God had a plan for us that only time would reveal.

A professor at Biola, Dr. J. O. Henry, invited us to fellowship with a new church, Calvary Baptist in Monrovia, where he was pastor. We were taken into the heart of those people with love and understanding.

We had very little money. We were in our own house but we had to make payments. We had money left from what Art had earned with TWA but we had to be very careful about spending it. We weren't sure of where our next penny would come from. We could not afford a telephone. With food, shelter and a small wardrobe we must be content. Our diet consisted chiefly of carrots and canned cornbeef hash plus apricot and strawberry preserves which I made from fruit grown in our yard. Art's mother had moved to San Diego to be near Art's sister. Her house was rented and we sent the money to her every month.

Art worked on a few temporary jobs. Florence Spencer gave him work refurbishing some rentals and other folks had short term jobs for him. The church was enlarging its facilities and Art helped there, too.

We wrote letters to many friends and relatives about our desire to serve as missionaries. We visited churches to tell about Radio Station HCJB and the ministry we would have in Ecuador.

Art would not go alone so I always went with him. We showed films and slides about the ministry and sang gospel songs. Our daughters went with us at times although they preferred staying with Virginia Wilson, a neighbor. She taught them how to do crafts.

After seventeen months of deputation ministry we had almost reached our goal. We lacked fifty dollars a month. The quota established by the mission was less than $400 a month. That included airplane fares, living allowance, rent, utilities, insurance, Social Security and incidentals. And I was pregnant again, which was the reason we lacked fifty dollars. That amount was required for baby support.

A family in Fullerton, the Leo Williams, came to interview us. We did not tell them the amount of money we lacked or why. After chatting a while, Mr. Williams asked, "How would you like for us to support your unborn child?" We were surprised.

"That would be great!" we replied. Then we told them that the fifty dollars was all we needed. Our quota was reached! We rejoiced together.

Unplanned at that time, the Williams supported that baby for many years longer than Art and I worked with the mission. When she was twenty-two she became a missionary with Campus Crusade for Christ and the Williams continued to support her.

In mid-December, 1952 we crated our household goods and other possessions and rented our house to friends. We shipped the crates to New Orleans where they would be stored until we finished language school, after which they would be shipped to Ecuador.

The mission required that new recruits attend language school in Costa Rica for a year. The nationals with whom we would work spoke Spanish and we had to learn their language so we could communicate with them.

On Christmas day, 1952 we landed in San Jose, Costa Rica. A fine missionary family, Southern Baptists, met us at the airport. They helped us find a house to rent and settle in. The new semester would begin in ten days.

To communicate with the Costa Ricans was difficult because we didn't know Spanish but we communicated as best we could with gestures and the few words we knew.

A week after we arrived I visited an American doctor with the mission hospital in San Jose. She took my blood count and discovered I was very anemic. She was worried about me having a Caesarean section with my blood count being so low. She said that if I hemorrhaged during surgery I might not survive. I must build up my blood immediately to an acceptable level for surgery.

My baby was due in seven weeks.

Meanwhile language school started. Daily I took a bus to classes after which I took a different bus to the hospital for a blood building injection. This routine soon became too strenuous for me and Art learned how to give the injection and saved me the trips to the hospital. After several more weeks the doctor tested me again. I still wasn't doing well. The doctor asked if some students at language school could give me blood transfusions. Art found several volunteers who had my type.

When transfusion took place, blood passed directly from the veins of the donor into my veins as it had done when my father gave me blood. However, after two transfusions the doctor discontinued them. She was worried that blood given when I was not losing blood might cause complications.

My blood count never reached the desired level but on February 12, 1953 I started labor and had to have the surgery. The president of Costa Rica was the chief surgeon.

Everything concerning the operation went well.

"It's a beautiful little girl!" stated the surgeon. He spoke English very clearly. Then he asked my doctor, "What did they want?"

"A boy," she answered.

"Women, what would we men do without women!" came the jovial response from the surgeon. I can still remember smiling as the anesthetist injected medication that caused me to sleep.

The baby, Rebecca Rose, was taken care of around the clock in the nursery. However no nursing care was provided for me during the night. A family member had to stay with a new mother. Art stayed the first night but he was so exhausted that he slept all night. He didn't wake up once despite my calling. He was very apologetic the next morning and I survived.

The baby was six weeks old when I resumed studies at the language school.

Janice attended second grade in an English-Spanish school and did well in both languages. We hired a local woman to stay with Gloria and Rebecca while I was in classes. Gloria played with the children next door and learned Spanish much quicker than Art and I did.

Art was adept at many things but not at learning a foreign language. He needed continual help. I was the only person readily available to work with him and we struggled together.

Costa Rica is a tropical paradise. I was not able to take excursions to various sites but Art, Janice and Gloria did, and they exclaimed about the beauty of the land, the volcanoes and rural areas.

Art and I were supposed to attend Language School one year but when we were halfway through our course an urgent request came from the directors of HCJB. All missionaries with our organization should fly to Ecuador as soon as possible. The Ecuadorian government had granted us visas and we had to accept them soon or we might lose them. Visas weren't easy to obtain during those years and we thanked the Lord for them.

In August, 1953 nine HCJB missionaries and our eight children boarded a plane in San Jose and flew to Quito.

Ten staff members were at the Quito airport to meet us. The staff at that time consisted of forty missionaries and an equal number of Ecuadorian employees. Gene and Ruth Jordan, talented musicians, were our hosts.

We stayed in Quito only long enough to refresh ourselves and eat dinner, after which a missionary drove us to the transmitter site that was destined to become our home.

The trip required one hour on cobblestone road that was narrow, bumpy, curvy and dangerously close to the edge of mountains.

The forty acre site on which we would live was twelve miles from Quito near a small town called Pifo. A transmitter building had already been constructed there. It housed several low-powered transmitters which carried messages and music over the air waves. New transmitters and antennas would be designed and constructed. Three homes had been built and missionary families lived in them. We had come to help them.

That drive to the site was an exciting introduction to a trip that we'd be taking several hundred times during the next twelve years.

SEVENTEEN

Transmitters and Tall Antennas

I was ready for almost any kind of existence. I had heard stories about how missionaries dwell in jungle huts, suffer deprivation and are isolated among people whose culture is very different from theirs. I thought I might find myself and my family living under similar circumstances.

To my surprise a two story brick house complete with fireplace and modern conveniences, such as electricity and a bathroom, was under construction for our family.

In the distance on all sides were breath-taking snowcapped mountains with fluffy clouds floating over the peaks. Tall slender eucalyptus trees bordered the property. The weather was pleasantly comfortable year round, never too hot and never freezing, like a day in spring. We were located near the equatorial line at about 8,000 feet altitude. Three missionary families who already lived there were: the Turrells, Beoughers and Wittigs. Among them they had six children.

Our house wouldn't be ready to move into for several months. Havana and Phil Turrell invited us to live on the second story of their house until ours was done so we moved in. There was no kitchen facility on that floor so my family took meals with the other missionaries. We had breakfast in one house, lunch in another and dinner in a third. The round robin eating helped us become well acquainted. Two of the men, plus Art, had served in the military during World War II.

Radio programs were transferred from the Pifo site to all parts of Ecuador and to various countries around the world such as Russia, Sweden and Germany. Programs were broadcast in six languages and were inspirational, educational and entertaining. Diesel generators provided power to run the transmitters. They also supplied electricity for the shops and our homes.

The mission's goal was to expand its outreach into all the world and to add other languages to the format. To achieve this more powerful transmitters and antennas had to be built and more broadcasters who spoke other languages were needed. The goal of the engineers was to design and construct the technical equipment that was needed. Art had come to help.

Diesel generators were already in place. The cost of fuel was expensive, however, and their output limited. The men dreamed that someday a hydroelectric plant would be built to generate power.

The engineers worked with great perseverance to make the goals a reality. Their first project for increased power was to build a 100,000 watt transmitter. They worked long, hard hours to design and construct it.

Some of the components that were needed had to be produced "from scratch" using materials that were on hand or available locally. Other components had to be ordered from the States or Europe, which frequently required a month of waiting.

Lighting struck an antenna near our house in Pifo.

As well as doing design and construction on new jobs the men had to maintain transmitters and antennas that were already on the air. At times some malfunction caused an interruption in broadcasting. The men worked day and night to repair whatever was faulty. The diesel generator broke down several times and had to be repaired. Transformers became faulty and had to be rewound. That was one of Art's specialties. The engineers taught competent nationals the art of the trade. More than a half dozen local men worked with them.

When Art had time for relaxation, he and I walked to the town of Pifo to visit families of national workers and to become acquainted with other townsfolk. When Art wasn't available one of my daughters or a friend walked with me.

One of the missionaries, knowing that my ability to communicate in Spanish wasn't very good, told me that conversing with people before I had a good grasp of the language might be detrimental to the work. She said I should probably wait until I had a better grasp of the language.

I replied that there was little that I could do in the ministry and that visiting was one thing I could do.

She and I decided that we needed counselling so we invited a pioneer missionary from Quito, Faith Turner, to visit us. Faith concluded that even though our communicative ability might not be perfect, if we showed love and an interest in the people, good would undoubtedly result.

Havana had been teaching a women's Bible class for a year but she was so pressed attending sick people who came to her door that she felt she could no longer teach the class. She asked me if I would take it and I accepted.

I still lacked proficiency in Spanish and was perplexed as to how I could communicate so that the Ecuadorian ladies would understand. I devised a plan: at the beginning of each week I read the lesson aloud in Spanish into a tape recorder. Then I listened hour after hour to my recording and memorized the sentences as best I could. I looked up words in the Spanish-English dictionary that I didn't know.

After much practice I could speak the lesson pretty well when I presented it to the class. A problem arose, however, when the ladies asked me questions. I couldn't understand them! They seemed to talk so fast! Fortunately Havana came to the class for a month and she answered their questions. Finally I was able to understand them well enough to reply. I added quilt making to Bible teaching and gave pieces of material to the ladies for attendance. They loved that and started making their own quilts.

The house that was being built for my family was finished in November. However, our crates from New Orleans had not arrived despite the fact we had ordered them to be shipped to us many months ago. The shippers informed us they had shipped them but now no trace of them could be found. Art and I had no household goods or furniture but the missionaries generously loaned us what they could.

Almost weekly for the next three months our mission office in Quito contacted the shipping company and customs office but no one seemed to know where those boxes were. Finally in February, 1954 the good news reached us that our boxes had been found in the customs warehouse in Guayaquil. They would be sent to us immediately.

We were delighted and excited when we received the possessions that we had crated more than a year earlier: washing machine, refrigerator, beds, household items, Art's tools, my typewriter, a baby buggy and clothing. The baby had outgrown some of her clothing but other babies could use them. Two boxes were missing and never found.

One of our first large purchases was a piano which we found "by accident" in Quito. The owner accepted our offer of a down payment and a half dozen promissory notes. The piano was on the third floor of an old building and had to be lowered down through a courtyard. This job required four men. They had to remove railings and bind the piano with ropes. They used a block and tackle to lower it. That was quite an experience!

Our salary was not large but it was adequate. Art and I felt we should spend as much money as possible on the cultural and spiritual development of our children. However, that wasn't the only reason we bought the piano. We wanted it for sheer enjoyment. I even taught a few nationals how to play simple melodies.

On Thursday afternoons a Bible class was held for employees. Several men received Christ as their Savior. Soon we realized we needed to hold Sunday services for anyone who wanted to attend. In April our first Sunday School class was held in the transmitter building. Sixty-five people were present and two recent converts were baptized.

Attendance increased weekly and within six months we realized we needed a church building.

In partnership with the nationals we missionaries designed a plan that would double as a Christian day school for their children and a church. It took us nearly two years to acquire enough funds to construct the building but we finally did.

Meanwhile the needs of the local people for medical attention increased greatly. Folks for miles around came to the HCJB compound because they heard there were ladies there who would help them. My three missionary associates, Havana, Kathryn and Keitha, were overwhelmed day and night by people with medical problems. They treated them on their doorsteps. Many people walked long distances. Others were carried in the arms or on the back of a loved.

Door step medicine

None of our missionaries were nurses by profession but they could not refuse helping people in need. Frequently they contacted our missionary doctors in Quito by telephone for advice.

Some patients were so ill that they could not come to the mission compound. A family member would ask our ladies to drive to see the sick person. Among our families we had only one vehicle, a carryall van. The ladies would drive to visit the patient, often over very rough roads. At times the missionary helped deliver a baby. Many calls were made to huts that had no electricity or running water.

Some cases could not be handled by our Pifo staff. Our men took turns driving very ill persons to our mission hospital in Quito. Usually the wife of the missionary accompanied him as well as the family of the patient.

I helped little in this ministry although I did accompany a missionary when I was needed and I assisted wherever I could. I even administered doorstep medication when missionaries were gone.

After several years of handling numerous cases, the missionaries asked the mission to send a medical doctor to our compound once a week to see patients. Thus began the clinic ministry in Pifo.

A doctor came every week. Some-times two doctors came. Always there were dozens of people waiting to be seen by them.

We had no clinic building. The only available space other than our doorsteps was the dismantled body of a bus. How well I remember Dr. Ev Fuller, who was 6 feet tall, crouched uncomfortably in a four foot space treating patients. He never complained.

A National evangelist always came with the doctors. He talked with each patient about the most important

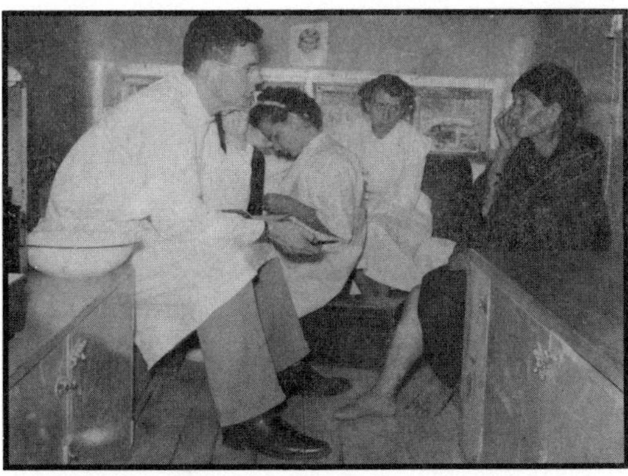

Dr. Fuller, his wife Liz and Kathryn Beougher attend a patient.

need: that of the healing of the soul through God's provision of salvation through Christ Jesus. Some believed and lives were transformed.

We missionaries soon realized that the circumstances under which these doctors worked was unsatisfactory. They needed a clinic building. United, we missionaries presented the need to our board of directors but a drive was being made for funds for a new, large hospital in Quito and the board felt that no other medical project should be announced at that time.

We missionaries decided that the need was so great that we would contribute funds from our salaries to build a clinic. We purchased all the materials such as cement, bricks, lumber, windows and a door. Our mission director permitted us to use some of our employees to help with construction. Our husbands worked on it, too, especially with the wiring, and within months we had a small, though adequate, clinic building.

The medical ministry grew more rapidly after we had a clinic building and soon we realized we needed a full time nurse on staff. Martha Brunner, a registered nurse, joined us. She did a marvelous job. Through the years she broadened her ministry to reach hundreds of persons with medical needs and she established her own maternity clinic in town.

Seeing the needs of babies whose mothers could not keep them, Martha accepted twenty into her home to become her children. After that she built a large mission school for Ecuadorian students.

When a missionary family went on furlough to the States, new personnel came to Pifo. The Whitakers, Lintz, Jacobsons and Ridgeways were among missionaries who lived and worked in Pifo during the time we were there.

The years spent at the transmitter site were perhaps the happiest in my marriage. I loved the ministry. I had freedom to do the work God had created me to do: serving, teaching, writing and broadcasting as well as rearing my children and maintaining a home.

Our children lived at home most of the time although they had to leave on Monday mornings to attend school in Quito, where they spent five days in a boarding home. Every Friday they returned to Pifo to be with us.

Marge prepares a manuscript at home.

They delighted in the broad expanse of the transmitter site. They went horseback riding, walked in the irrigation ditch, climbed hills, picked wild flowers and, of course, did their tasks around the house with a little prying. They shared friendships with both Ecuadorians and Americans.

Art was challenged by the projects. He spent many hours each day in the transmitter building helping design and construct transmitters, repairing electronics equipment and doing tasks related to broadcasting.

There were incidents of conflict, however. He did not always agree with his fellow workers on certain aspects of the work. Art complained vigorously not only to me but to them. He got angry because a plan he designed had been questioned and some decisions didn't go to his liking. Frequently he would come home angry. Occasionally he would

Art at work in the transmitter building.

tell me to start packing. We were going home to the States and never come back. However, after a while, he would calm down and return to the transmitter building.

Many visitors came to Pifo to see the work being done there. We missionary ladies hosted people by the dozen. We each had a helper in our home, without whom it would have been impossible to accomplish what we did. The noon meal at my house sometimes included three to ten visitors. There were no restaurants within miles of where we lived.

On occasions groups from Quito had picnics on the property. Several times more than a hundred persons came. They brought their own refreshments.

We hosted afternoon teas for visiting Americans, foreigners, officials of the Ecuadorian Government and Army, evangelists, musicians, engineers, broadcasters, local people, U. S. Point Four personnel and priests.

Our close knit Pifo group celebrated all holidays with festivity. In some ways we were transplanted Americans but in many ways we weren't. We dug our roots deep into Ecuadorian culture and loved the country and its people.

At times we encountered opposition from townspeople, especially when we started holding church services in nearby villages at the request of new believers. Stones were thrown at our vehicle. Antagonists set up road blocks and initiated rallies to harass us. Mobs sometimes gathered to block our way. These occasions were infrequent and we always escaped unscathed.

Although we suffered no physical harm, several hundred miles distant in the jungles of Ecuador five missionaries met death on January 10, 1956. They were martyred by the Auca Indians. All had visited our plant in Pifo. Their spiritual influence had been great upon us. We grieved in disbelief.

The widow of one, Betty Elliot, needed a small transistor receiver. Art and two engineers, Herb Jacobson and Kermit Beougher, worked three days and nights virtually without sleep to design and finish the project. Betty used the transmitter at her jungle station to maintain instant contact with her mission base.

Furlough time arrived for us in August, 1956. We flew to Miami where we bought a used car and drove to Kansas City.

We arrived in California in time to enroll our daughters in school. Art worked on a temporary engineering job for nine months and on Sundays we visited various churches to tell about the work of HCJB in Ecuador.

EIGHTEEN

We Return

After nearly a year in the States we returned to Miami in our used car. On our way we visited friends and family in various areas and were able to see the Grand Canyon, Niagara Falls, the Yankee Stadium and the Empire State Building. We sold the car in Miami and flew to Ecuador.

Life in Pifo resumed its busy and exciting pace. Art worked in the transmitter building and I kept busy at home and among the people.

For Art's forty-second birthday I baked an angel food cake. Recipes for baking cakes in the altitude have to be adjusted with less of some ingredients and more of others. I forgot to make the adjustments. The cake fell and it looked like pudding. Art was gracious about it. He said he liked pudding.

The girls presented him with a gift wrapped in decorative paper and sealed with black electric tape. When he opened the package and saw pajamas and socks, he grinned and remarked, "You've been in the barrels already!"

Living out of missionary barrels was a way of life. Before we left the States we always tried to acquire enough clothing and gifts to last three or four years. Of course we weren't successful, but the barrels supplied a lot.

While we had been in the States, Janice learned to play the viola and now wanted to learn to play the violin. We were able to get excellent teachers for her. One of the teachers was from France. When he returned there he shipped us a fine violin.

A man from a nearby village, Yaruqui, came to our plantel to request that someone come to his town to hold services. Art and I consented to go and Sunday afternoons found us in a house in Yaruqui. One of our national workers preached. Art lead singing and I played a portable pump organ. Our daughters helped with music and drama. They enjoyed participating in the services and conversing with children their age.

Every summer our family took a vacation for two weeks. We traveled by train and bus to the coastal city of Guayaquil. Art and I were frugal and made our sucres (the Ecuadorian word for dollars) stretch as far as they could. We did things that the common people did and went places where few Americans went. In Guayaquil, a large coastal city, we attended a Russian ballet. In Quito we heard the U.S. Airforce Band and the New York Philharmonic Orchestra.

I had always loved to write poetry and articles and decided to take a correspondence course in journalism. The first story I wrote was published in a major Christian magazine and later in a book of best stories. Before long I had many stories published.

Staff members in Quito started giving me writing assignments. I wrote scripts and edited a monthly news report about our missionaries and their ministries. Also I was offered my own half hour program weekly. I called it "Designs in Living."

Missionaries need to maintain a vital link with their supporting family and friends. The main avenue by which they do that is through letters. One of my tasks was to maintain that link. We liked to include our children in our letters and the recipients seemed to enjoy hearing about them.

When Janice was nine I wrote, "Jan is getting so big and pretty and her teeth are coming in nicely. Her talents are much like her father's but she is more reserved. She is so sensitive she wouldn't dare do anything bad."

About Gloria and Becky I wrote, "Gloria is not quite six and she takes life as it comes and goes, with never a thought that is confused. If I punish her for wrongdoing she cries a while and then sings or whistles and probably forgets the punishment. She does try to be a good girl most of the time."

"Becky, almost two, talks all the time, is always hungry, eats a lot and is very active. She sometimes carries her filled potty to me."

Gloria hated to wear shoes and removed them as frequently as possible. In one year she lost two shoes from different pairs in the stream close to our house.

One day Gloria poured sand over her head and told me she was washing her hair. When she learned to play jacks she wanted to do it all the time. While taking a bath she put them in the bathtub and bounced the ball to pick them up.

The girls grew up to be quite style conscious. They wanted to wear pretty dresses, which sometimes was hard to fulfill because we had to depend a lot on what was in the barrels. They also wanted their hair to look nice.

During summer vacation Gloria and Becky planted onions and carefully tended them. One day they decided the onions were ready to eat so they invited four little neighbors to share the honor of harvest. Six smelly kids entered my house.

"You've been eating onions!" I declared as I guided them out the door.

It is doubtful those children would have eaten raw onions at the dinner table but none could withstand peer pressure.

Janice read a Bible passage to me one day. "Noah was just a man," she read. The Bible, however, says he was a just man! I laughed at her interesting reversal.

Another time I read the story of Ruth and Naomi to the girls. I told them how Naomi had changed her name to Mara. Gloria, age six, asked, "Mother, when I was a little girl, was my name always Gloria?"

The girls wanted a full explanation of what a mother-in-law is so I told them. Afterwards, Gloria prayed for her mother-in-law!

I read the ten commandments to them including "Thou shalt not make any graven images." I asked Becky to repeat the verse. She said, "Thou shalt not make any gravy."

Art took turns working at night in the transmitter building and the girls argued over who was going to sleep with me since Daddy was gone. Sometimes I'd wind up with two of them. They snuggled so close that I would almost fall out of bed. I would have to get up and walk to the other side to find space.

During summer vacation the girls and I worked on a schedule of their activities during the day. We stated the hours they would practice their instruments, make their beds, wash supper dishes, read the Bible, ride the horses and play. The schedule was seldom adhered to as planned, but it did help organize their tasks as well as determine rewards or punishment.

Some folks wonder what missionary kids do. We had animals to take care of: a dog, chickens, rabbits, a pig, two horses, a lamb and even bees. Each girl had her own garden spot.

They painted Christmas cards, did embroidery work, tanned rabbit hides, read books, pitched a tent and helped with Vacation Bible School, an annual event. Girlfriends visited them from Quito. Janice went to Youth Camp on the coast.

When Becky was two and a half years old she experienced an inflammation of the trachea which caused her to breath very rapidly and stressfully. We rushed her, under oxygen from a tank in the transmitter building. to the hospital in Quito. She recovered but similar incidents occurred at least twice a year until she was five years old. The last occurrence was the most severe. She stopped breathing. Missionaries gathered for prayer and God healed her. The illness never occurred again.

One of Art's special abilities was rebuilding transformers. If a transformer quit the power in the transmitter had to be lowered. The outreach of the broadcasts was limited. At times the damage was so bad that the transmitter had to be shut down and no programs could be carried on that transmitter until the transformer was repaired.

A damaged transformer had to be rewound as quickly as possible and pressure was exerted to get the job done. One transformer weighed 1500 pounds and required two weeks to rebuild. The work was very detailed. Art insisted that he be the only person to do the rewinding. He feared that someone else might ruin the motors. The work was very tiring but he always got it done successfully.

One day a worker, Enrique Toinga, touched a 2,200 watt transformer which was alive by error. He bounced off since it was direct current but he struck it again and bounced off again. He was badly burned in two places and stopped breathing. Art administered artificial respiration. Enrique breathed again. Another missionary gave him oxygen and then drove him to the mission hospital in Quito.

We ladies prayed and cried before the Lord for his recovery. He made a remarkable comeback and within two weeks was on the job again. Ultimately he became a highly successful technician.

NINETEEN

Panama Plus

During the summer of 1960 a request came from our sister station HOXO in Panama. An engineer was needed to help upgrade their transmitters. Could they borrow an engineer from our staff for one year? He could bring his family with him.

Art accepted the assignment. We had been in Pifo three years during our second term and were due a furlough to the States. We agreed to stay in the States only a few months after which we'd go to Panama.

While in the States we bought a Rambler station wagon. In July 1960 we drove it on the Panamerican Highway wherever the road was passable through Mexico, Guatemala, El Salvador, Honduras, Nicaragua and Costa Rica. We pulled a box trailer behind us. It was loaded with supplies we'd need in Panama plus tools and equipment for the station.

That trip was the most rugged we ever experienced. The road was fairly good until we reached southern Mexico. At that point the road was washed out for a hundred miles due to flooding from torrential rain. There was no way we could travel farther south except by train. We had to load our station wagon, trailer and family on the flatbed of a freight train. The train made forty stops during the eight hours we were on it to load and unload merchandise. The frequent stopping and starting made the trip very jerky.

My family and I detrained at times and boarded again before the train pulled out of a station. At one point, however, Janice, who was sixteen, missed boarding the train. We panicked when we saw her below us waving wildly and screaming. I started screaming, too.

Art was about to jump off the train when he saw two men kneel down at the far end of our flatbed. They extended their arms downward in an effort to grab her hands. However, they couldn't reach her in time. They yelled to some men on the end of the flatbed that followed ours. Those men knelt down, stretched their arms and were able to grab Janice's hands. They swung her upward onto their platform. Fortunately the train wasn't moving very fast.

We expressed our gratitude to all the men who helped. They didn't seem to think that they had done anything unusual. Maybe it wasn't for them but it certainly was for us. Art would have jumped off the train had his daughter been left behind. Later we noticed that men and boys missed the train at times and hopped on board without fear.

Finally we reached the end of the line. We were assured that the road was in good enough condition for driving. However, it was unpaved and very winding at times. We hit lots of ruts and more than once our vehicle came close to running off an embankment.

We traveled many miles without seeing buildings or people. At several points we passed children walking in the road. That was an indication to me that homes must be nearby.

While traveling in Guatemala the trailer came apart. The wheels and axle dropped off from underneath the trailer and rolled to the side of the road. The bed of the trailer dragged behind us for a few feet.

Now here we were stuck in a barren area with the bed of the trailer in one place and the wheels in another. Art was patient, however. He determined what he needed to repair the trailer. Leaving me and the girls by the road with the stuff, he drove to the nearest town. By chance and God's provision, it was only a few miles away. There he sought the parts he needed and was informed that missionaries lived in the village. Before long he brought a missionary with him who helped rebuild the trailer. We all loaded it and that night we slept in the headquarters of a mission.

Ten days after we started our trip we arrived in Costa Rica and we discovered that the highway ended there. No road existed to Panama. The only way we could get to Panama was either take an airplane or a boat. We decided that Art would go by boat with the car and trailer and the girls and I would fly.

Art dismantled the trailer and loaded it and the contents inside the station wagon. Having one vehicle to ship was cheaper than having two. A day later the girls and I flew to Panama. Our family was happy to be reunited and to have reached our destination. Thus began our year's stay in Panama City.

Life here was very different from life in Ecuador. The weather was hot and humid. Food was expensive. Housing was costly and rentals were scarce. Our first home was in the suburbs far away from town. The girls had to take two collectivos, the open air buses, to reach school and that made me a bit nervous. Within a month we found an apartment closer to town. We moved. However, we were still too far from schools so we started looking for another place. Within a month we found an apartment that suited our needs. We moved three times in three months. Fortunately we still had the box trailer.

The last apartment was in the heart of the city where noise seldom abated until midnight. Cockroaches were our constant companions wherever we lived in Panama and the more we destroyed the more they seemed to multiply.

The only recreational activity we could enjoy without perspiring profusely was swimming. The YMCA in the Canal Zone permitted us to use their pool. Since we were not military personnel everything was off base to us except the pool and the enlisted men's cafeteria. We visited both once a week.

We came in contact with a few Americans but most of our friends were Panamanians. I found it difficult to understand their dialect but Art's ears picked up sounds more keenly than mine. I'd asked him, "Are they speaking Spanish or English?" "Creole," he'd answered.

We attended the Iglesia Central on Sunday mornings and the Salvation Army services at night. The Captain of the Salvation Army, his wife and three sons became our closest friends.

The Salvation Army sponsored an outing for 450 Panamanians. Art and I and the girls went, too. Eight busses transported our group to a beach on the northern coast. Art and I helped dispense food and drink. We worked four hours without a break. Art's job was hard because he had to pop metal caps off hundreds of bottles. However, he enjoyed it. It gave him an opportunity to greet every person and to converse with many.

During summer vacation, one of the churches held Bible School for two weeks. The director asked me to teach the boys and girls how to pray in Spanish. I outlined simple concepts about prayer and taught them to begin with, "Nuestro Padre Celestial." Then I asked the children to name some blessings that they were thankful for. They couldn't think of anything except Mama or some family member. I knew that their blessings were few yet I asked confidently, "You can thank God for your house, can't you?"

"No," they responded.

"Why not?" I asked.

"We don't live in houses," came the reply.

"Oh, that's right!" I replied. "Well, you can thank Him for your apartment."

Heads shook negatively again. "We don't live in apartments."

"Where do you live?" I asked.

They all answered, "In a room." One girl added, "All we have is one room."

Another child stated that twelve people lived in her one room. We thanked God for one room and I realized anew how fortunate I was to have a two bedroom apartment. Noisy and hot as it may be, it was large and luxurious compared to what they had.

Our daughters were permitted to attend school in the Canal Zone because we were U.S. citizens and we paid tuition. The girls found the studies more demanding than they were in Ecuador or in the States but they made good friends and seemed to be happy. Except for the heat.

Art went shopping for groceries. One day he saw some boxes filled with unlabeled cans. The grocer said he didn't know what was in the cans. If Art wanted to buy them he's sell the whole bunch for $4.95. Art paid the price and brought home five boxes of we-didn't-know-what. We counted eighty cans!

We surmised that cans of equal size contained the same product so we stacked them in that order. Our assumption, however, was wrong. Many cans held something different from what we expected. The opening of cans became a game. We never knew what we were going to have for dinner until we opened a can. There was more pork and beans than anything but we also got peas, corn, soup, pineapple juice, tomato juice, peaches, milk and meat. One can contained caviar. None of us liked it but we found a family that did so we gave it to them.

Ice cream was bountiful in Panama. We ate it almost daily. Art found a wholesaler who produced a variety of flavors in five gallon containers. We ate the same flavor for several weeks each time we bought it but we enjoyed it.

In July, 1961 our year in Panama came to an end. We sold our car and trailer to missionaries who needed them. Personnel at HOXO told us they were happy we had come. Art had helped them a lot with their transmitters. Even I had contributed. I had helped with writing scripts and broadcasting.

We left Panama with tears in our eyes and lumps in our throats. What we thought might be a dull year proved to be a colorful one. Living in Panama had its problems but also it was adventurous and fascinating.

We had furlough time due us so we returned to California for six months. We bought a 1953 Ford for Art which cost $235. and an older Chevrolet for me costing $100. It was the first time I had my own car. Neither car gave us any problems.

Art got his old job back on temporary assignment. The money he earned helped greatly with our outgoing expenses.

I took a television writing course at U.C.L.A. and Jan studied violin with a distinguished teacher who lived near the university.

We sold my car for the price we paid for it and drove the Ford to Miami where we sold it for $200.

On our flight to Ecuador we deplaned in Panama for a two day visit. That was the last time we ever stepped foot on the territory of American soil in the Canal Zone.

TWENTY

ॐ

Adios Ecuador

Pifo was a tranquil, pastoral scene quite in contrast to Panama City. We had been absent two years and were happy to return to our adopted homeland.

The work in the transmitter building had progressed well. The church gained attendance and our national school had fifty boys and girls in attendance. Four of the children walked five miles each morning to come to school.

Every school day we missionary ladies fed the children milk and bread, which we baked. Two Ecuadorians were teachers and we helped them. I taught Bible, English and music.

Art resumed former duties and was assigned new tasks. Television had come to Quito, introduced by our mission as HCJB-TV. Art helped construct and erect antennas for the TV station in Quito. I wrote programs in Spanish for a weekly telecast for children.

A project that was in its initial stages was the construction of a hydroelectric plant. Land and water rights had been purchased about fifteen miles from Pifo in the town of Papallacta. The main purpose for the plant was to provide increased electrical power.

I resumed jobs which I had before we went to Panama. A new task, however, was teaching Becky piano lessons. She told me that I could teach her only one year.

"Why?" I asked.

"By that time I will know all you know," she answered. I don't think we lasted a year!

I also found myself fulfilling an unusual request: cutting the hair of Ecuadorian ladies. A young woman from the village named Lucia discovered that I cut my daughters' hair and my husband's hair. She wanted me to cut hers. I told her I had never cut hair anyone's hair except my family's.

She persisted. I reminded her that the men of her village forbade their women to cut their hair. For centuries long hair was a custom strictly adhered to. A man would be disgraced if his daughter or his wife cut her hair.

I told Lucia that I was afraid her father would get angry at me and also at her. She pleaded with me. I finally agreed that if she obtained permission from her father I would cut it. She left seemingly satisfied.

The next morning she returned assuring me she had her father's permission. I clipped. Cutting her thick, long hair wasn't easy but I trimmed it shoulder length.

Her father never came to rebuke me and the cutting of Lucia's hair appears to have set a trend in the village. Many women in Pifo starting cutting their hair, although, I'm happy to say, only a few came to me.

Some of the customs of the village people were similar to those which the pioneers of America practiced in the colonial days.

Shopping for beef in Pifo, Ecuador.

The butchering of animals was done in courtyards. Chunks of meat were cut from carcasses and sold on the spot.

Cows were milked in pastures where we went with our milk can to buy what we needed. Live chickens were brought to our doors. After purchasing one, we had to kill it by cutting its throat, pluck its feathers and remove the entrails. We, too, did some tasks the way pioneer women had done.

A spinner of yarn in my front yard.

Indigenous women of the area wore long dresses and shawls. There was little variation in the style or color of their clothing. Skirts and shawls were dark blue or black. Blouses were white with embroidery around the neckline. The women wore many strings of beads. Some women came to our door spinning raw wool on a shuttle, thus turning it into thread.

Often they brought eggs for us to buy. We were never certain of what the egg might be like inside. Some eggs had been in a nest too long and when we cracked it, the stench was putrid. However, most eggs were alright. Despite the fact that all seemed to be fertile it didn't matter if they weren't too old.

Other victuals such as bananas and vegetables were brought to our door and we bought them. At times I'd ask the vendor if he or she ate some of the vegetables which they grew.

Many times the vendor would answer, "No, we don't eat them. We just sell them."

That would stir me to present a few words about the value of eating vegetables and not just selling them. Maybe it did some good. I'm not sure.

Few homes in the village of Pifo had more than one forty watt light bulb. Power for electricity was provided by a small diesel generator in the town. One of the villagers maintained it. Some haciendas owners also had diesel generators. All too frequently the generators broke down. Bob Wittig, our diesel engineer, helped many of these men with repairs.

In December, 1962 my father became critically ill from cancer and was given a few weeks to live. He wanted me to be with him during his last hours. My parents would pay my round trip fare to Kansas City if I would come.

Arriving at his side I spent four precious days with my Dad. He wanted to be certain that God had forgiven him of his sins. He said he had been a great sinner and felt unworthy of heaven. Yet he said he had a firm faith in the Lord. I assured him that because of his faith in what Christ had done to save him eternally, he would be in the presence of God. Dad surrendered peacefully. A week after the funeral I returned to Ecuador.

Art and our daughters fared well while I was gone but after I returned Art had moody spells worse than ever before. He complained about his fellow workers and the work being done. He and the other engineers sometimes differed in their opinions concerning designs, construction and maintenance. At times Art came home angry. He would tell me to pack. We were leaving for the States. However, he would calm down shortly and return to the job.

Art also had increasing differences with our daughters. They wanted to stay in Quito occasionally on weekends. They had been invited to a party or a school program or a student activity that wasn't held during the week. Art said emphatically that they could not stay. They must come home where they belonged.

Gloria especially wanted to be involved. She was invited to sing in a trio and had to turn it down. I tried interceding to Art but he became angry. His children had to be at home where they belonged. Despite his declarations he did permit them to stay in Quito several times. Also he urged them to bring friends to Pifo.

Janice complained the least. She was more submissive to strict regimentation. Anyway, she liked to ride her horse and read books.

In the spring Janice finished high school. She stayed with us during the summer. During that summer something profound happened in her life. Tom Baker, a student in his senior year at Massachusetts Institute of Technology came to Pifo as an intern and spent three months. He worked on innovating projects, lived with one of the missionary families and ate meals with all of us.

Tom and Jan developed a friendship. Romance blossomed. In September Tom returned to MIT and Jan flew to the west coast to attend Biola.

The Larson family in 1964.

After Jan left, Gloria became very discontent. She was lonely on weekends without her older sister. She and Becky grew closer, however.

I began thinking about Gloria and Jan not returning with us after our next furlough. Both would remain in the States in college. Becky and I would be alone with Art. That made me apprehensive. How could I manage life with him, without my two girls?

Many times when Art was angry he told me that he wanted to leave and I began wondering if our ministry in Pifo was finished. I didn't want to resign from the work permanently, however, and wondered if we might be able to work in Quito. Art could work in the studios. I could become more involved in writing and programming. I would enjoy living in Quito.

However, when furlough was due in 1965, Art decided that we should take a leave of absence. I had a premonition we would never return.

We sold most of our possessions and took what was left in suitcases on the plane. The saddest one to leave was Becky. Ecuador was home to her.

I could not say goodbye to Ecuador without taking part of it with us. Art and I' invited a lovely twenty-one year old Ecuadorian, Sara Martinez, to travel as our guest. She was eager to visit America. Her brother, Jorge, had been in the States for several years.

In May, 1965 we flew out of Quito. Arriving in Miami we made our usual trip across the States and settled in California. Within a few weeks Art went to work as chief engineer of Radio Station KBBI in Los Angeles.

Six weeks after our arrival a wedding took place. Jan and Tom Baker were married. She was a lovely bride and Art and I were delighted to have this brilliant young engineer and devout Christian as our son-in-law.

The Baker family, 1994.

TWENTY-ONE

The Ultimate Journey

Three months after we arrived in California the Watts Riot, a racial conflict, tore at the heart of South Los Angeles. Art was working with Radio Station KBBI in downtown L.A. Many people telephoned the station about their fears and asked for prayer.

Thirty-five persons died in the conflict, hundreds were injured and $200 million was done in damages.

Our home was about twenty miles from the afflicted area.

Another clash that had started in 1964, the Vietnam War, lasted nine years. Eight million American servicemen went overseas, many never to return home. Millions of Vietnamese suffered loss. The war was proposed to preserve a separate independent non-Communist government in South Vietnam. Finally a peace agreement was signed.

Gloria attended Biola College then moved to Loveland, Colorado where Jan and Tom were living. At the Presbyterian

The Elijah family in 1990.

Family photo, 1976. Taken four years before my mother died. Heather Baker, lower right, at the onset of her fatal disease.

Grandma Marge with Maria and Marta, 1975.

Church she met Vietnam veteran Vern Elijah and they were married in June, 1969.

For sixteen years Art and I lived in Southern California and worked at interesting jobs. He was chief engineer of several Christian radio stations and I worked as a writer for Moody Institute of Science, The Ungame Company and Fuller Theological Seminary. I worked at the video console of Christian T.V. I attended Cal State University and received two degrees in Communications. Becky graduated from college and became a missionary to Europe. She met Peter Pohle, a fellow missionary and artist from Berlin, Germany. They were married in 1982.

Our three daughters and their husbands had nine children, two of whom, Maria and Marta, were adopted from Ecuador.

Our first grandchild, Keith Baker, was born in Loveland. He was our delight! Fourteen months later his sister, Heather, arrived.

She was a normal, bright child until age seven when the disabling effects of a rare genetic disease appeared. Metachromatic Leukodystrophy was progressively debilitating and eventually lethal. The strong witness of Tom and Jan of the love of God during those years was manifested in their care of their invalid daughter. Heather died at age twenty-one.

Art and I moved to Loveland, Colorado in 1981 where we built a passive solar house. We returned to Ecuador for a visit and traveled in other countries.

In May, 1987 Art and I visited friends and family in Florida and Georgia. One night he became violently ill and we headed for home the next morning. Art needed medical attention but he wanted to get home to Colorado before seeing a doctor.

Never before had Art permitted me to drive more than a few miles but now he was happy to have me drive hundreds of miles. He was barely able to keep alert.

After two days of driving we arrived in Loveland. Immediately Becky informed us that she and Peter, her husband, and two children had to leave for California the next morning. They had a job opportunity that they must fill within a few days or lose it. They also needed someone to drive a van pulling a trailer.

Everyone in the family was too busy to help them drive to California except me and Vern's nephew. Peter pulled a trailer behind his car and I pulled a trailer behind mine. The two thousand mile round trip to California took me three days.

Becky and Peter Pohle and daughters, 1993.

Meanwhile Janice and Gloria and their husbands looked in on Art and Janice took him to the doctor's office. They did not get any report about his condition even thought they telephoned the doctor's office daily. Eventually they found out that the doctor had gone on vacation.

Another doctor in the same office took his case and made extensive tests on Art that took four hours in the hospital. Immediately the doctor told us that tests indicated that Art had cancer of the pancreas.

Art and I hardly knew what this meant except that the doctor told us the illness was serious. He said Art had three options concerning treatment. He could choose the one he preferred. He could have radical surgery which would require five hours or more and from which he might not survive. Or he could choose not to have surgery which would mean death possibly within weeks. Or he could have a surgical bypass with the possibility of extending his life for a year or more. Art chose the latter and told the doctors that his faith in Christ sustained him and that death for him meant eternal life in the presence of God because he trusted the Savior.

Surgery was performed and Art remained quite active for several months. He built an amplifying system for our church with the help of Dick Martin. This was a project he had planned and wanted to finish above all else.

Art's seventieth birthday was on July 23 and we celebrated it with refreshments at the church for the entire congregation.

At home, Art frequently hummed the song "I Walked Today Where Jesus Walked." The words comforted him. He decided he wanted to share his testimony with the congregation of the church and to sing the song. On August 2 he had the opportunity to do it. He related several ways the Lord had blessed him, then with full volume and without falter he sang. Although he had become unsteady during his three months of illness he stood unaided and remained firm.

My daughters and I could not hold back the tears. As soon as he finished we walked to the rear of the auditorium to console one another.

I realized that Art had a terminal illness but I believed he would live a year or more. Nevertheless tears welled in my eyes at times despite my resolutions to restrain them. One day I asked myself, "What's wrong with me? Why do I grieve? Aren't Christians supposed to be models of stoic piety?"

I confided in our pastor, Jim Murphy, and he said that Jesus wept. "Weeping is an emotion God had provided for us to release pent up sorrow," he said.

After that I felt more comforted when tears stung my eyes although I brushed them away as best I could.

I didn't want my husband to die. Living with him had not been as agreeable as I had hoped a marriage would be but I loved him and admired his talents. He was interesting, adventurous, generous. Almost every day he told me he loved me. During frank discussions we had about our relationship the only comment he usually made was that he was disappointed with himself.

The greatest comfort I had during Art's last days was the realization that through faith in Christ we will live eternally.

During times of weakness I received comfort through reading the Bible and listening to cassette tapes of the Scriptures.

Art wanted to visit Becky and her family in California. He also wanted to see close friends and family members who lived there. The doctor forbade him to take the trip but on August 6, 1987 Art and I boarded an airplane destined for the state of his birth. I had written loved ones from south to north and all of them came to see us at Becky's apartment.

After we returned home to Loveland Art spent most of his time in bed. He always mustered sufficient strength to converse with anyone who visited him. On the evening of August 17 he called me into his room to say he was sorry he had not been victorious over his temper. He said that before he received Christ he was frequently out of control. Christ had made a difference in his life but Art regretted that he had never conquered his temper as he should have.

As a child, when he became angry he would bang his head on the floor. He didn't want to but he couldn't keep from doing it.

Art said he was telling me this because he was very sorry. I answered that he had victory at times and he replied, "Not really."

"Maybe you have a physical problem that caused you to react as you did," I suggested.

To that he would not respond. All his life he felt that conduct such as his was due to a lack of spirituality. Nothing more or less. He downgraded the possibility that he may have physical or psychological problems.

Art and I grew up in an era during which mental problems were looked upon as disgraceful. Persons who had mental problems were called "crazy" and a stigma was placed on their family. Many persons with mental and psychological illnesses were institutionalized as incurable.

A spiritual problem was considered quite differently. The person who had one could overcome it by trusting God and doing right. I felt Art's problem was psychological but every time I suggested seeking help he rebuffed me.

Art had been an unwanted child. His mother had hoped her baby would be a girl because two years earlier she had lost a small daughter with pneumonia. She refused to give her new son a name and told a nurse she could name him. The nurse named him Arthur for her brother who was a soldier in World War I and Glen for Glendale, the city where he was born.

On August 21, 1987 Art and I went to the doctor's office for a checkup. Art was so weak he could hardly stand and he had lost more weight. The doctor told us, "You need not come again." Neither one of us dare ask why.

I slept in a room adjoining Art's during the last month of his illness. During the nights of August 25, 26 and 27 Art made groaning noises and I could not sleep. I was so exhausted by August 28 that I asked my daughter, Gloria, to stay with her father until midnight so I could get some sleep. She could go home at that time since with a little rest I could stay awake the rest of the night.

At 8:30 p.m. Vern, Gloria's husband, came to the house. After conversing I asked him when Gloria was coming. He said, "She isn't. I'm going to watch Art tonight."

I went upstairs to sleep. At 1:20 a.m. I awoke, concerned about Art. I walked downstairs and into his room. Vern was still awake and said Art was fine. He also said that one thing he was learning was that TV isn't worth looking at after midnight. I returned to bed but I couldn't sleep. I went downstairs again.

Vern said that Art had called for me and he told him that I was sleeping upstairs. Art had groaned and Vern had taken his hand. Vern is a jovial, quick-witted fellow. He said that Art looked at him as though he were saying,. "Well I guess you're better than nothing!"

I told Vern that I was alright and he could go home. He said, however, that he was going to spend the rest of the night with us and that I might as well go upstairs. I did but again I could not sleep. I came downstairs and checked Art. He seemed to be sleeping well.

Vern and I conversed quietly at his bedside. Within minutes Art's breathing became shallow. Then he let out long gasps.

"Why is he doing that?" I asked.

"I don't know," Vern replied.

I soothed Art's forehead. Then I held one of his hands. It was cold. "Art has never had cold hands," I remarked. Instinctively I uncovered his feet. They were cold. "His feet have never been cold!" I exclaimed. "I don't understand this!"

Despite all the instructions I had been given concerning the symptoms of death, I was totally unprepared to recognize them. Vern looked for Art's pulse. "I can't feel any," he said.

Then we looked at Art's chest to see if he was breathing. There was no indication that he was.

For moments I seemed to be in outer space. Art was dead. I experienced a sensation as though I were conscious yet, at the same time, lacked consciousness and was being carried by a power outside myself. I was in shock. It took me some minutes to recover.

I was grateful that Vern was there. He was strong, tender and considerate.

I telephone Art's nurse. She came right away.

Vern called Gloria. She came, broken with tears. I was grateful that Gloria had been spared seeing her father take his last breath.

Jan and Tom were traveling home from Arkansas where they had taken their freshman son, Keith, to enroll at John Brown University. Before Jan had left Loveland she was apprehensive about going but I had assured her that her father would not die during that time and that Keith and Tom needed her.

At about ten a.m. the morning of Art's death, Jan, while passing through Kansas City, telephoned to find out how her Dad was. When I told her that he had died, she fainted at the telephone. For what seemed like minutes I shouted her name and finally I heard a faint whisper, "We'll be there as soon as we can."

Through the years my brothers and their wives had been loyal friends. They hurried from Arizona and Missouri to be with me and my family and to attend the funeral.

The memorial service was precious. Dr. Jim Murphy, our pastor, gave a brief biography of Art's life. Then he presented an invitation to anyone who did not know the Saviour to come to Christ, as Art had asked him to do. Our eight year old grandson, David, sang a solo . After the service Bill Warnock said to me, "That's the kind of service I'd like to have when I die." I considered his statement a beautiful tribute.

Burial was in Whittier, California with a graveside service for friends and loved ones there.

Days to follow were difficult but I buried myself in activities and in the reading of God's Word.

The death of a loved one does not finalize life for his survivors although at times it may seem to do so. Nor does it bring activities to a halt. Life continues. Mine did so at a fleeting pace.

TWENTY-TWO

Life After Death

I was glad I didn't have to live alone during my first year of widowhood. Janet Bright, a friend, lived upstairs for several months. After she left Gloria and her family lived there until I sold the house.

Art had bought me a double wide mobile home before he died. It was an ideal home for a widow, except that it needed a lot of repair. Art planned on doing the work but became disabled sooner than anticipated. The home had been empty a year. Water lines had bursted and all types of work needed to be done. The task of refurbishing fell upon me and it was great therapy.

I hired a plumber, carpenter, drywaller, roofer, electrician and solar specialist to do various jobs. My son-in-law Vern helped. Two high school boys and I assembled kitchen cabinets.

I purchased all materials, traveling to Denver, Fort Collins, Greeley and Loveland. I was grateful that Art had taught me a lot about home construction. The responsibility was taxing but also it was therapeutic. The work occupied my mind and time for several months and I had little time for prolonged grieving.

However, after all the jobs were done and I was alone I found my thoughts continually turning toward the loss of my husband.

At bedtime I fell asleep rather quickly but after a few hours I would awaken suddenly. Confused dreams centered around Art's death and I couldn't fall asleep again. I tried to quieten my mind by praying and listening to Bible portions on cassettes. That helped yet sleep was still far from me.

To remain in bed became more taxing than arising so I'd get up and do some work in the house until I felt exhausted. I did wallpapering and organizing during those late night hours.

After a month of this insidious midnight disturbance I began wondering if my sleep pattern would be interrupted forever. It wasn't. Within another month my sleep was restored to a near normal pattern.

A widow finds herself doing many little jobs that she had not done before her husband's death. Mine included mounting car license plates, removing and replacing door knobs, changing a battery in a fire alarm and doing yard work alone.

As long as I had plenty of work to do and slept well at night, I made it successfully through each day during those first months.

I missed Art's help in many tasks but I missed him most when I used my computer. He had rescued me many times from problems in word processing. Now I had to look to someone else for help. Tom, my son-in-law came to my rescue.

Finally all the remodeling was finished and, being alone, I had time to think. And a new hurt surfaced. I encountered an aspect of sorrow that I had not anticipated. It is called anger. I was not angry at God but at my deceased husband. Things he had done to me and my children popped in my mind. The pain I had felt then I felt again.

Why had Art been so accusative even in non-essential matters? And why had he been so loud in his accusations?

I was angry because Art had been accusative and temperamental. But, I asked myself, why did I recall things I wanted to forget? Why was I so bitter? I felt guilty for having such thoughts and yet I didn't seem to be able to get rid of them.

Why wasn't I able to forget the hurt the children and I had suffered? I knew that somehow I must and yet I didn't know how to do it.

I had never discussed our irascible relationship with anyone although at times friends and relatives initiated conversation about their concerns. I always made superficial replies and no one pressed me for answers. In reality, I was too proud and too ashamed to admit that we had a problem.

Now, months after his death, I was not mending well. I wanted to forget unsavory occurrences but I couldn't.

Through Elderhostel, an outreach to senior citizens, I heard about a one-week counselling program at the Narramore

Christian Foundation in California. Persons who desired counselling from a Biblical perspective were invited to attend. I knew I needed help. I asked three of my lady friends to attend the sessions with me and they did.

Professional guidance was given through lectures in classrooms and on an individual basis. Attendees had the opportunity to take part in a counselling group. I was the first person in my group to unburden my problem. As I confessed the difficulty I had forgetting and forgiving, I told them of various occasions when Art's explosive accusations had been so severe that I was wounded emotionally. I told how the intense anger of my deceased husband returned to my mind at times and I could not forget or forgive.

As I talked I wondered if the folks in my group could believe me. Or would they think my imagination had gone wild?

I was amazed at their responses. And happy. Yes, they did believe me. They knew I needed help. They didn't condemn me. They didn't even scold me. Several said they had experienced similar situations but not as difficult as mine.

The counselor stated, "It is possible for you to overcome your problem. The way to do it is to forgive your husband and to tell him so."

He said that I should have told my husband about my hurt before he died and have forgiven him and have told him that I forgave him. Now, despite the fact that he was gone I needed to forgive him and to confess my forgiveness to him and to God. I should tell Art that I forgave him forever. Then I must bury all hurt, disappointment and anger in love, and trust God to help me forget it.

In the solitude of my room that day I did as the counselor advised. I confessed. I begged pardon. From that moment onward I have experienced peace.

When Gloria, my daughter, read the script of this book she stated, "Mother, you portray yourself as cool and indifferent toward Dad. That was never true. You suffered a lot because of his temper and so did we children. When you mention it was hard for you to forgive him, someone may ask, 'What did he do that was so awful.' Mother, you don't mention actual incidents."

I reply, "It's all gone. I have forgotten most and have forgiven all."

Many adventures marked the years when Art was alive. We traveled a thousand miles around Australia in a Greyhound bus for 28 days, not knowing for certain where we would lodge at night. We climbed down the 40 foot shaft of an opal mine. We saw koalas and kangaroos in the wild, slept in an underground motel, talked with aborigines.

In New Zealand we discovered that the numbers on the telephone dial run the opposite direction from those in the U.S. We visited the native Maories there. In Hawaii we ate poi, went snorkeling, attended a luau and saw the Kodak hula show.

We visited Germany several times and worked in a mission there for a month.

I was counselor to groups of students travelling overseas and have visited every continent except the South Pole. I rode on a camel in North Africa, walked the Via Dolorosa in Israel, visited Pompeii, entered many castles in Europe. I made a train trip with my mother from Vichy, France to Nurnberg, Germany that required eight changes in trains one way. Yes, we did get lost! I traveled England, Spain, Scotland and Wales. I have ridden on the underground, double deck buses, school buses, taxis, bicycles – most any mode I could find for transportation. I've walked a lot, too. London, which requires a lot of walking for sight-seeing, is one of my favorite cities.

Now in my seventies I ask, "What can I do of value?" Also, I question, "Will I live long enough to see my grandchildren marry and have children?"

Whatever comes, I know that my life will be chock-full of surprises. An earth moving one took place two years ago. I met Melvin Sinks, a retired farmer, widower and fine Christian. Our wedding was a big celebration hosted by my daughters and their husbands.

It's never too late to begin again!

Marjorie and Melvin Sinks, 1992.

ða

Through The Years

This chapter enumerates events of history, customs and and happenings in America and around the world during the 1920's to the 1990's. Listed are occurrences and people best recalled by the author: a nucleus for future development.

Events and people of the 1920's:
PRESIDENTS: 1913 to 1921: Woodrow Wilson
1921 to 1923 Warren G. Harding
1923 to 1929 Calvin Coolidge
1929 to 1933 Herbert Hoover
VICE-PRESIDENTS: Thomas Marshall, Calvin Coolidge, Charles H. Dawes, Charles Curtis
AIRFLIGHT: Charles Lindbergh makes first solo flight nonstop from New York to Paris
AIRPLANES: first planes licensed to carry passengers
AUTOMOBILES: new Fords, Dodges, Cadillacs, Packards, Mercedes Benz
CHAIN STORES: J.C. Penney, Western Auto, Safeway, Woolworth, A & P, Sears Roebuck and other new ones
CAPITOL PUNISHMENT: Death in the electric chair
CREDIT: Easy Payment Plans to purchase almost anything
FAMOUS PERSONALITIES: Louis Armstrong, Clara Bow, William Jennings Bryan, Richard E. Byrd, Al Capone, Lou Chaney, Charlie Chaplin, Charles Darrow, Jack Dempsey, Duke Ellington, Bobby Jones, Greta Garbo, George Gershwin, Red Granger, Al Jolson, Joe E.Lewis, Sinclair Lewis, Charles Lindbergh, Tom Mix, Eugene O'Neill, Knute Rockne, Will Rogers, Babe Ruth, Aimee Semple McPherson, Alfred Smith, Billy Sunday, Gene Tunney, Rudolph Valentino, Johnny Weissmuller, Paul Whiteman and others

FASHIONS: Shorter skirts, bobbed hair, corsets, scanty bathing suits, raccoon coats

GANGSTERS: Mobsters, racketeers, speak-easies, bootlegging

MAGAZINES: *True Confessions, Good Housekeeping, National Geographic, Life, The Saturday Evening Post, Collier's*

MAIL ORDER HOUSES: catalog advertising made products available by parcel post to your door

MUSIC: Syncopated sound, jazz, the blues, negro spirituals, big band orchestras, 78 rpm records and victrolas

ORGANIZATIONS: Rotary, Kiwanis, Chamber of Commerce, Lions, Elks, Ku Klux Klan, etc.

PROHIBITION: January 16, 1920 the 18th Amendment made liquor illegal throughout the country. Enforcement difficulties, moonshining, graft. Amendment repealed thirteen years later

RADIO: has practical beginning for John Q. Public (the populace.) First sponsored programs broadcast in New York. 6.5 million radio sets purchased by 1925

SLOGANS: became popular such as "Quick, the Flit!" and Maxweli House's "Good to the Last Drop"

STOCK MARKET: October 24, 1929 the stockmarket crashed. Stocks lost more than 40 per cent of their value.The economy was unsound and banks weak. Catastrophic for Americans, the Great Depression began

TABLOIDS: Newspapers about half the size of the ordinary newspaper and with more photographs and controversial subjects became popular during this era

THEATRES: By 1922 weekly theatre admissions totaled forty million. By 1927 there were twenty thousand theatres in the United States

THEOLOGIANS: Reuben E. Torrey, C. I. Scofield, William Erdman, Billy Sunday, Dwight L. Moody, Paul Rader. First radio broadcast of a church service, 1920. In 1922, 348 religious stations were in operation and 732 broadcast in 1927

TRAVEL: Tourist courts, mobile homes, Burma Shave signs

YOUTH: Flagpole sitting, yo-yo's, marathons, mandatory chapel attendance abolished at college, first Miss America contest, slick hair style for males, the Jazz Age and a moral revolution

Events and people of the 1930's:
PRESIDENTS: Herbert Hoover 1929 to 1933
                     Franklin D. Roosevelt 1933 to 1945
VICE-PRESIDENTS: Charles Curtis, John Garner and
                     Henry Wallace
ANIMATION: The first animated film fantasy "Snow White and
     the Seven Dwarfs" in 1937 is huge success
AVIATION: First helicopter flight
COMIC STRIPS: Little Orphan Annie, Dick Tracy, Tarzan, Buck
     Rogers. Tarzan was created by Edgar R. Burroughs for news-
     paper, then daily radio serial and movies. Buck Rogers did
     amazing exploits in imaginary 25th century outer space
DEBS: Glamour girls from wealthy families had coming out
     parties. Barbara Hutton, the poor little rich girl, married
     two counts and divorced
DIRIGIBLE: Airship German Hindenburg bursts in flames in
     New Jersey
DUST BOWL: Spring and summer, 1937 huge dust storms move
     across central and southern states causing great devastation
ELECTRICAL APPLIANCES: now available to all: irons,
     mixers, vacuum cleaners, washing machines, sewing
     machines, lamps and shavers
EVANGELIST: Aimee Semple McPherson
GANGSTERS: John Dillinger, Baby Face Nelson, George
     "Machine Gun" Kelly, Pretty Boy Floyd, Bonnie and
     Clyde, Ma Barker and her boys
GOVERNMENT: F. D. Roosevelt, 32nd president March 4,
     1933, developed New Deal, NRA (National Recovery
     Admin.) CCC (Civilian Conservation Corps), WPA (Works
     Progress Admin.) and PWA (Public Works Admin.) Henry
     Wallace was Secr. of Agriculture; Harry Hopkins, Secr. of
     Relief; Harold Ickes, Secr. of Interior; J. Edgar Hoover,
     Director of the FBI
GREAT DEPRESSION: Thirteen to fifteen million unemployed:
     twenty five percent of the working force. Thousands home-
     less. Poverty was a way of life for many
KIDNAPPING: Lindbergh's 20 month old son abducted and
     slain by Bruno Hauptmann March 1, 1932

MEDICINE: First blood bank established, first artificial heart
    experiment

MOVIE STARS: Tom Mix, Mickey Rooney, Jane Withers,
    Jeanette MacDonald, Nelson Eddy, Clark Gable, Will
    Rogers, Marie Dressler, Janet Gaynor, Joan Crawford,
    Robert Taylor, Jean Harlow, Gary Cooper, Bette Davis,
    Fred Astaire, Ginger Rogers, the Marx brothers, W.C.
    Fields, Shirley Temple, who at age five in 1934 made her
    first movie. Six million Shirley Temple dolls were sold

MUSICIANS: Big Bands, Swing Bands: Benny Goodman,
    Tommy Dorsey, Jimmy Dorsey, Artie Shaw, Bob Crosby,
    Glen Miller, Count Basie, Duke Ellington. Vocalists:
    Bing Crosby, Helen O'Connell, Billie Holiday, Marion
    Hutton, Ella Fitzgerald, The Andrew Sisters

NYLON: DuPont Co. in Delaware in 1939 manufactured new
    fabric called nylon, heralded in the use of dozens of
    synthetic products. One example: detergents

OLYMPICS: 1932 in Lake Placid, New York and Los Angeles
    California. In 1936 in Berlin Jesse Owens, U.S.A won
    five gold metals

PRICES: steak 29¢ lb, pork chops 20¢ lb, margarine 13¢ lb,
    bread 5¢ loaf, sugar 5¢ lb, cornflakes 8¢ a box, new shoes for
    man $1.79, bed sheet 67¢, 9x12' wool rug $5.85, bicycle
    $10.95. Six room house in Detroit with garage $2,800. in
    1932 to 1934. Gasoline about 20¢ a gallon

RADIO: Four networks captivated American audiences. FM
    radio invented. Radio Personalities: Fibber McGee and
    Molly, Ozzie and Harriet Nelson, George Burns and Gracie
    Allen, Jack Benny and Mary, H. V.Kaltenborn, Kate Smith,
    Amos 'n Andy, Our Gal Sunday, Edgar Bergen and Charlie
    McCarthy, Kay Kyser, Major Bowes, First Nighters, One
    Man's Family, Gangbusters, Flash Gordon, Jack Armstrong.
    By 1932 eight percent of all radio programming was
    religious. First missionary station founded in Ecuador in
    1932 by Clarence Jones and Reuben Larson

RENOUNCED: The throne of England by Edward VIII of
    England for Baltimore divorcee Wally Simpson

SCIENCE: Origin and advances in radar, atomic research, TV, diesel-electricity, florescent lighting, helicopter flight, jet engines, parking meters, ball point pens

SHOCK RADIO: Orson Welles, October 30, 1938, presented radio play "Invasion from Mars." Script simulated news broadcast of invasion forces from Mars landing in New Jersey and devastating with death rays

SQUATTERS: Hundreds of World War 1 vets squatted near capitol in Washington several months until forced away. Many migrant workers moved to mid-west and western states to find jobs harvesting grapes and other crops

UNIONS: John L. Lewis, leader of the United Mine Workers, fought for rights of laborers to join a union. Unions organized with difficulty

WAGES: Annual wage in early thirties: $2,391 for dentist; $3,382 for medical doctor; $1,227 for public school teacher; $1,040 for secretary; $8,633 for Congressman

WAR: Sept 14, 1938 Britain's prime minister Chamberlain negotiated with Adolf Hitler over German claims on Czechoslovakia. In 1939 Germany declared war on Poland. England and France declared war on Germany. U.S. tooling up for defense

WORLD FAIRS: 1933-34 Chicago International Exposition: "Century of Progress." 1939-40 New York World Fair "World of Tomorrow"

YOUTH: drug store soda fountains, arched eyebrows, saddle shoes, hats, 4-H clubs, gimmick and giveaway seekers

WORLD INVOLVEMENT IN WORLD WAR II 1940 to 1945:

1940:

Battle of Britain: Germany invades England. Royal Air Force conquers. Nazis retreat

Battle at Dunkirk, France: Allied troops lose ground to Germans

Norway and Denmark invaded by Germany

Russia defeats Finland

Selective Service Act passed in USA

1941:

Hitler declares war on Russia. Nearly reaches Moscow.
Japanese make surprise attack on Pearl Harbor:
> 1500 Americans killed, 1500 injured, U. S. declares war.

Japan strikes at Philippines, Hong Kong and Malay.
British Navy sinks Russian Bismarck

1942:

Gen. Douglas MacArthur leaves Philippines with oft-quoted "I shall return!"

Malta suffers worst air attack of the war. British Royal Air Force loses 146 planes.

Allies surrender in Luzon, Philippines. Twelve thousand Americans among 75,000 prisoners forced to march to camp a hundred miles away. Many die on march.

Gen. James Doolittle raids Tokyo and three other Japanese cities with sixteen U.S. B-25 bombers

War is full flung on various fronts including South Pacific, North Africa and much of Europe. In New Guinea, U.S. Navy planes inflict heavy losses on Japanese.

Thousands of Japanese-Americans are interned to inland camps away from their homes on the west coast of U.S.

1943:

Russia joins the allies (U.S. England, France, etc.)
Soviets recapture Kiev and move toward Leningrad.
German forces pull out of Tripoli, North Africa.
U.S. Navy survives battle in Tarawa, island in Pacific.
President Roosevelt meets with Prime Minister Churchill of England and Premier Stalin of Russia in Morocco. They agree on invasion of Sicily, Italy and France and the continued bombing of Germany and provision of supplies to Russia

1944:

Heavy fighting continues.
D-Day in Normandy of northwest France.
Western allies invade Nazi occupied France and liberate Paris. Nazis overwhelmed U.S. troops in Luxembourg but two weeks later U.S. troops stopped the Germans in Belgium at Battle of the Bulge.

Germany rains rockets on London.
Allied and U.S. troops move in Italy and liberate it.
In South Pacific U.S. Navy, at full strength, wins in bloody
    battle near Japan

1945:
Triumphant Marines raise the U.S. flag on Iwo Jima, a South
    Pacific Island pertaining to Japan.
Allies invade and conquer Nazi Germany. Germany
    surrenders in May.
Japan surrenders Okinawa in June.
U.S. atomic bomb destroys Hiroshima and Nagasaki, Japan
    in August.
World War II ends with Germany signing peace treaty.
Hitler commits suicide as do his leaders Himmler and
    Goebbel. Mussolini is executed.
Mass graves of Nazi victims are found at Nordhausen

HOMELAND HAPPENINGS DURING WAR YEARS

1940 to 1945:
PRESIDENTS: Franklin D. Roosevelt 1933 to 1945
VICE-PRESIDENTS: John Garner and Henry Wallace
G. I. JOE: Draft boards established across USA. Draftee notice:
    "Greetings! You have been selected…" Induction Center,
    immunizations, 1/2" hair cuts, fatigues, basic training, USO
    entertainment, base chaplains, instant soluble coffee popular
    with armed forces later becomes popular with civilians
CIVILIAN DEFENSE: During four years of war the government
    stopped the manufacture of every item whose materials could
    be used in the war effort. Most household items and autos
    were no longer produced. Food was rationed. Stamp books
    issued with point value assigned to foods. Housewives paid
    grocers with rationing stamps as well as cash. Victory
    gardens sprung up: civilians grew vegetables to combat
    shortage. Grease rendered from meat was salvaged, metals
    and newspapers were collected. Gas rationing began in July,
    1942. Red Cross women rolled bandages, emergency blood
    banks were founded and plasma provided for servicemen

INTERNMENT: Americans of Japanese descent were given 48
     hours to dispose their businesses and to report to one of
     fifteen internment centers where they spent the duration.
MEDICINE: Sister Kenney develops polio treatment. First
     patient is treated with penicillin in 1941
SONGS: Popular wartime songs: Praise the Lord and Pass the
     Ammunition; Don't Sit Under the Apple Tree; You'd be
     so Nice to Come Home To; This is the Army, Mister
     Jones; When the Lights Go On Again
TAX: Congress approves withholding tax and the term "take
     home-pay" was adopted in 1945.
TV: New York City telecasts in black and white as first
     commercial TV station, 1941. Beginning of color TV
     appears in 1945
WAR EFFORTS: Aircraft, naval ships, cargo ships, artillery,
     small arms and ammunition, bombs, tanks, guns,Jeeps and
     other vehicles were produced by civilian workers

Events and People of 1946 to 1949:
PRESIDENT: Harry S. Truman 1945-1953
VICE-PRESIDENT: Allen Barkley
AUTOMOBILES: Return to making cars in 1947
APPLIANCES: 1946 first electric clothes drier, garbage
     disposals and automatic dishwashers
BLOCKADE: American and British forces fly thousands of tons
     of food and supplies daily to Berlin due to blockade
     Soviets placed on Berlin
COMPUTER: A computer 50 feet high in four story building,
     and 100 feet long was introduced in 1949
COMMUNISTS: Eleven leaders of U.S. Communist Party are
     convicted under Smith Act
EDUCATION: G.I. Bill provides higher education for
     servicemen
EVANGELISTS: Charles E. Fuller, Carl Henry, Jack Wyrtzen,
     Percy Crawford, Oral Roberts, William Bright, Irwin Moon,
     Walter L. Wilson, Youth For Christ begins. Billy Graham
     preaches to 30,000 people in Los Angeles tent 1949:
     6,000 converted

INVENTION: Electric blanket is invented
FILMS: Gone With The Wind, produced in 1940, still popular.
    Moody Institute of Science produces Christian films
FLIGHT: First jet plane takes off from an aircraft carrier
GOVERNMENT: The Marshall Plan spurs European postwar
    recovery with U.S. financial aid. Truman Doctrine
    provides immediate aid for Greece and Turkey. Taft
    Hartley Act anti-trade union passes over Truman's veto.
    USA organizes N.A.T.O. Alliance. President Truman
    makes first telecast from the White House
ISRAEL: British mandate expires in Palestine and Britain pulls
    out. Jewish leaders proclaim new nation of Israel with
    David Ben-Gurion as Prime Minister. Five Arab states
    attack Israel but are defeated
MEDICINE: Cortisone and neomycin discovered
MUSICALS: Oklahoma! and South Pacific. Composers: Hart
    and Rodgers, Oscar Hammerstein, Allan Jay Lerner
OLYMPICS: First since 1936 are held in London
PERSONALITIES: Douglas MacArthur, Roy Rogers, Doris Day,
    Rita Hayworth, Betty Grable, Tennessee Williams, Frank
    Sinatra
RADAR: First radar signals from USA are bounced off a satellite
    240,000 miles away
RADIO: Singing commercials
RECORDS: RCA and Decca sold 100 million 78 RPM and two
    years later plastic 45 rpm and long play 33 rpm were new
    on the market
SPORTS: Joe DiMaggio, Babe Ruth, Jackie Robinson, Joe Lewis
    and Gorgeous George. Kon-Tiki raft made of balsa wood tied
    with hemp sails 4,000 miles in the Pacific manned by
    six Norwegians
YOUTH: Juke boxes, jitterbugging, drugstore milkshakes, fair
    paying jobs, acne, drive-in theatres, car hops, roller
    derbies, home perms, conformity: most youth are
    responsive to traditional parental discipline

Events and people of the 1950's:
PRESIDENTS: 1945-1953 Harry S. Truman
                        1953-1961 Dwight D. Eisenhower
VICE-PRESIDENTS: Alben Barkley and Richard Nixon
ART: Commercial art, avant-garde artists
BOOKS: The Holy Bible sold 2 million copies in 1952, also best
    seller next two years. Encyclopedias popular and children's
    books
CIVIL RIGHTS: Negro seamstress refused to give her seat on
    bus to white man in Montgomery, Alabama, Dec. 1, 1955.
    Martin Luther King met with Negro leaders to organize non
    violent boycott. King's home bombed. Supreme Court
    declares bus segregation illegal in Alabama. In 1954 Supreme
    Court orders public schools to integrate. In 1957 Eisenhower
    sends troops to Little Rock to enforce Court decision
CUBA: Gen. Fidel Castro invades Cuba
DEFENSE: Atomic Energy Commission founded. H-bomb
    tested. Obliterated one Marshall Island. Radio activity 25
    miles in the air
FADS AND FASHIONS: Hula hoops, contact lens, mid-calf
    dress-length, full skirts, shorter shorts, sack dresses
FILMS AND FILM STARS: Tony Curtis, Janet Leigh, Grace
    Kelly, Debbie Reynolds, Eddie Fisher, Elizabeth Taylor,
    Marilyn Monroe
FOOD: outdoor barbecues became popular; hot dogs,
    hamburgers, potato chips
GAS: 25 cents a gallon
GOVERNMENT: Senatorial investigation of Joseph McCarthy
    who claims long list of Communist Party members in
    U.S. Government. McCarthy condemned 67 to 22.
    Eisenhower called press conference in Abilene, Kansas
    in June, 1952. TV cameraman takes film: news reporters
    complain at the priority of that new medium
H-BOMB: Hydrogen bomb is tested in Bikini of the Marshall
    Islands by USA
HOUSING: More than 2 million 750 thousand new housing units
    were started in 1950 to 1960. Split level housing began.
    Bomb shelters were built by some civilians

KOREAN CONFLICT: U.S. involved three years in conflict, under United Nations. General Douglas MacArthur, Allied Commander. 116,000 U.N. troops killed including 54,000 Americans

MAGAZINES: *TV Guide, Sports Illustrated,* children's magazines, movie star magazines, horror comics, *Eternity Magazine, Christian Life, Moody Monthly*

MEDICINE: In Boston first successful organ transplant (kidney). First successful open heart surgery by Dr. F. John Lewis. First sex-change operation. First use of radio isotopes in medicine. Salk Vaccine, 1955, for poliomylitis.

MISSIONARIES: Five American missionaries are killed in Ecuador by Auca Indians: Jim Elliot, Peter Fleming, Ed McCully, Nate Saint and Roger Youderian

MUSIC: Pop. Rock 'n Roll. Eddie Fisher, Perry Como, Peggy Lee, Lena Horn, Mario Lanza, Tony Bennett, Julie London, Patti Page, Liberace, Mitch Miller, Harry Belafonte, Elvis Presley, Nate King Cole, Andrew Sisters, Dick Clark, Pat Boone

RECREATION: favorites seem to be camping, boating, bowling

RUSSIA: launches satellites, constructs atom bomb

SCIENCE: First living creatures (four monkeys) sent into stratosphere by USA. First satellite launched, Explorer I. First computers for commercial use are sold in USA. Electric power is produced from atomic energy. First laser patent is applied for. Flying saucers reported as spotted

SPORTS: Willie Mays, baseball

STATEHOOD: Alaska 49th state 1958, Hawaii 50th state 1959

STOCK MARKET: Prices jittery in 1957

TEEN REBELS: Murders 26% more in 1956 than in 1955, increase in auto theft, dangerous weapons, gang names and violence, criminal charges, switch blades

TV: Television is flickering tube at beginning of 1950's but improvement is rapid and TV becomes greatly used source of entertainment and information. Stars were Milton Berle, Dick Clark, Howdy Doody, Walter Cronkite, Dobie Gillis, Ozzie and Harriet, Father Knows Best, Leave it to Beaver, What's My Line, The Lone Ranger, Hopalong Cassidy,

Lassie, Space Patrol, Davy Crockett, Mickey Mouse Club, Kukla, Fran and Ollie, Gunsmoke, Wagon Train, Maverick, I Love Lucy, Your FBI, Dragnet, Gang Busters, Hallmark Hall of Fame, Studio One, Playhouse, Goodyear Playhouse, Philco Playhouse, Kraft Theatre, Steve Allen, Jack Parr, Dinah Shore, Edward R. Murrow. Color TV in 1955. Charles Van Doren fakes answer on quiz show "Twenty-One." Lawrence Welk, 1954

YOUTH: Little league, baton twirling, transistor radios
Collegian fad: 22 students pack in telephone booth
and more pack into a Volkswagon

Events and people of the 1960's:

PRESIDENTS: 1953 to 1961 Dwight D. Eisenhower
1961 to 1963 John F. Kennedy
1963 to 1969 Lyndon B. Johnson
1969 to 1974 Richard M. Nixon

VICE-PRESIDENTS: Richard Nixon, Lyndon B. Johnson,
Hubert H. Humphrey and Spiro T. Agnew

ASSASSINATIONS: President John F. Kennedy slain by Lee Harvey Oswald; Oswald shot by Jack Ruby before TV viewers; James Earl Ray assassinates Martin Luther King, Jr. Malcolm X, black activist, slain

ASTRONAUTS: Russia pioneers space flight in 1961. Alan Shepard, first American to fly in space. John Glenn, first American to orbit the earth. Neil Armstrong and David Scott made first space docking. Neil Armstrong and Buzz Aldrin, first men to set foot on the moon, 1969. Aldrin planted American flag on the moon. Spacecraft names: Mercury, Geminis, Apollo

CIVIL RIGHTS: August, 1963 200,000 persons marched on Washington D.C. demonstrating for civil rights. Martin Luther King speaks, "I have a dream." Act of 1964 bans racial and religious discrimination, segregation ends. Right to vote

COMIC STRIP: Snoopy and Charlie Brown

COMMENTATORS: David Brinkley, Chet Huntley

COMMUNICATIONS: Computers process data electronically,

storing the information, retrieving it and rapidly transmitting it as needed. Production multiplies rapidly and uses increase. TV and radio usage and print media also expand

EXERCISE: Jogging becomes popular

FILM STARS: Raquel Welch, Lana Turner, Diahann Carroll, Julie Andrews

GOVERNMENT: Doves and Hawks, The New Frontier (Pres. Kennedy's challenge to Americans), the Peace Corps founded

HOUSING: High rise apartments, residential communities for single adults, first retirement town for senior citizens

ISRAEL: 1967 Six Day War saw Israeli forces occupy the Sinai, Gaza Strip, West Bank, East Jerusalem and Golan Heights. Five years later gradual withdrawal from the Sinai

MEDICINE: Contraceptive: the pill. Pacemaker is developed in England. Genetics code DNA revealed. Medicare begins for retired U.S. citizens

MOVEMENTS: Women's Liberation Movement. Homosexual Rights Movement. The Jesus Movement

MUSIC: The Beatles, Rock 'n Roll, Rolling Stones, Joan Baez, folk singer

PERSONALITIES: Shirley Chisholm, Twiggy, Eugene McCarthy, Ralph Ginzburg, Dr. Benjamin Spock, Senator Barry Goldwater, Mayor Richard Daley, George Wallace, Eldridge Clever, Malcolm X, Jacqueline Kennedy, Senator Ted Kennedy's car plunges off bridge, his secretary drowns

RIOTS: 58 cities, including Watts in South Los Angeles, Cleveland and Chicago, exploded in riots in 1964-1967 leaving 741 dead, 4,552 injured, black ghettos burned, civil rights workers beaten, several killed

SCIENCE: First laser built 1960, Boeing 747 jet in 1969

SPORTS: Cassius Clay, Lew Alcindor, Arnold Palmer, Joe Namath, O. J. Simpson, Mickey Mantle, Jack Nicklaus. 1969 Olympics in Moscow

TELEVISION: Johnny Carson, The Smothers Brothers, Rowan and Martin, Flip Wilson, Jimmy Walker

WALL: Berlin Germany wall built by Communists to prohibit residents of East Germany to migrate west. Persons attempting to escape were shot

WAR: Vietnam War with thousands of American servicemen fighting overseas. Green Berets. Anti-war protests. Six-Day War in 1967: Israel seizes Sinai and Gaza Strip and regains Jerusalem

WEDDING: Jacqueline Kennedy and Aristotle Onassis 1968

YOUTH INSURGENCE: The Flower Children, Hippies, Love Children, Hare Krishna, Students for Human Dignity, Black Panthers, Yippies, psychedelic experiences, the drug cult, marijuana, group images, posters, feathers, beads, long hair, radical makeup, fluctuating styles in clothing, fishnet stockings, miniskirts, off beat colors, the Mod look, the funky look, Rock 'n Roll, Woodstock, New York where 400,000 young people gathered three days in 1969.

Events and people of the 1970's:

PRESIDENTS: 1969-1974 Richard M. Nixon
1974-1977 Gerald R. Ford
1977-1981 Jimmy Carter

VICE-PRESIDENTS: Spiro T. Agnew, Gerald Ford, Nelson Rockefeller, Walter Mondale

AIRCRAFT: Concord supersonic passenger plane is built. Worst U.S. air disaster: D-10 jetliner crashes in Chicago killing 275 people in 1979

ART: Pablo Picasso, Jackson Pollock, David Smith, artists

ATHLETES: Hank Aaron, Muhammad Ali, Jack Nicklaus, O. J. Simpson, Billy Jean King, Bobby Riggs, Roger Staubach, Nadia Comaneci, Chris Evert, Jimmy Connors, Mark Spitz, Evel Knievel

COMPUTERS: great strides in advancement of programmable electronic devices that store, process and retrieve data. Circuits in tiny chips of silicon. Computerized   check outs now in grocery stores

COST OF LIVING: inflation, recession

ENVIRONMENT: Environmental movements. Earth day. Protection of endangered species such as the whale. Nuclear power denounced

FILMS: Earthquake, Star Wars, Jaws, Roots, Holocaust, Airport, The Exorcist

FLOOD: Big Thompson Canyon, Colorado, 139 deaths

GOSPEL MUSIC: Ralph Carmichael, Bill and Gloria Gaether, Kurt Kaiser, John W. Peterson, Evie, Ira Stamphill, George Beverly Shea

GOVERNMENT: Nixon freezes wages and prices, takes dollar off gold standard. J. Edgar Hoover is chief of FBI. Independent U.S. postal service created. July 4, 1976: 200th anniversary of America's independence

HOSTAGES: Teheran, Iran: 90 people at American Embassy, including 63 Americans, taken hostage by militants of Khomeini demanding return of former Shaw. 52 Americans held hostage 444 days

KIDNAPPING: Patti Hearst, kidnapped by Symbionese Liberation Army, takes part in bank raid

MEDICINE: Test tube baby. Thalidomide produces deformed babies. Harmful effects revealed from smoking. Acupuncture popular. Abortion becomes controversial issue, Roe vs. Wade decision

MOVEMENTS: Doves and Hawks. Evangelical Protestant groups and charismatic Catholics show great growth. First annual Christian Artists Seminar. Falwell's Moral Majority

MURDER: Death penalty returns as constitutional, 1977. Murderer Charles Manson and three men guilty of Sharon Tate murder and six others.

NOBEL PEACE PRIZE: Henry Kissinger, U. S. Secretary of State. Mother Theresa 1979

NUCLEAR ACCIDENT: Three Mile Island in Pennsylvania has major nuclear reactor accident

OIL: Arab oil embargo 1973-74, oil prices double in America heavily dependent on OPEC, energy crisis, boom in sale of small cars, especially Japanese and German

OPERA AND BALLET: Luciano Pavarotti, Beverly Sills, Mikhail Baryshnikov, Martha Graham (modern dance)

PANAMA CANAL: President Carter signs treaty turning
     Panama Canal over to Panama
PENTAGON PAPERS: 7,000 page top-secret study of U.S.
     involvement in Vietnam
PERSONALITIES: Howard Cosell, Farrah Faucett-Majors,
     Jaclyn Smith
POWER: Nuclear power, solar power, windmill power. U.S. and
USSR sign five year treaty limiting size of underground nuclear
     testing
PREACHERS: Pat Robertson, Jimmy Swaggart, Jerry Falwell,
     Hal Lindsey, James and Tammy Baker, Charles Swindoll,
     James Dobson, Robert Schuller
PROTEST: In 1970 Kent State college students protest Vietnam
     War, burn ROTC building. National Guard opens fire, killing
     four students, wounding eleven. Five days later one hundred
     thousand students march in Washington D.C. in protest
RADIO: 20 hours or more weekly devoted to religious
     programming by 110 radio stations in 1973. Religious
     stations in 1979 number 449
SCIENCE: Silicon chips. Computer revolution. Lasers
     concentrated energy used in industry, surgery, science and
     holograph. New items: digital watches, video tape recorders,
     electronic games, electronic C.B. radios. First
     communications satellite Telstar provides live, world-
     coverage of events. The "black hole." New discoveries in
     astronomy. Solar energy, directly from the sun was being
     tapped for heat and other uses
SPACE: Apollo missions to the moon. U.S. Apollo docked with
     Russian spacecraft. Space shuttle developed. Moon landing
     using first lunar rover. Viking I and II set down on Mars,
     1976
SPORTS: hang gliding, wind-surfing, skateboarding, jogging,
     topless bathing on some beaches
TELEVISION: British Muppet show, All in a Family, Sesame
     Street
VIETNAM: Napalm attack on rural South Vietnam intended to
     rout hiding Vietcong, destroys lives and property. Peace
     accord signed 1973. North and South Vietnam unified with

Hanoi as capitol in 1976. U.S. Congress votes $405 million
for South Vietnamese refugees: 130,000 settle in USA
WATERGATE: Break-in of Democratic headquarters in
Washington D.C. by burglars trying to plant listening
devices. Tapes confirm presidential involvement and Richard
M. Nixon resigns as President
WORLD: Africa: newly independent states: Angola and
Mozambique. Guerrillas take control. Uganda dictator Idi
Amin; Denmark, Ireland and Britain form European
Economic Community (The Common Market); Iran: Shah of
Iran deposed, Ayatollah Khomeini reigns; Israel: Camp
David peace treaty between Israel and Egypt; Mexico:
Sandinista leaders; Nicaragua: Civil War ended 1979,
President Somoza deposed; South America: many countries
governed by military dictators; Soviet Union dominates
Poland and other allies
YOUTH: Skateboards, sweatbands, running shoes, T shirts,
layered look, designer jeans, skimpy shorts, varied hairstyles
and punk haircuts, torn clothing, folk patterns, leather coats,
fast food chains become popular, 18 year olds can vote.

Events and people of the 1980's:
PRESIDENTS: 1977-1981 Jimmy Carter
                1981-1989 Ronald Reagan
                1989-1993 George H. Bush
VICE-PRESIDENTS: Walter Mondale, George Bush,
                Dan Quayle
AIRCRAFT: Cruise missiles developed to fly beneath enemy
radar cover. Airplane explodes over Lockerbie, Scotland in
1988: 270 persons killed
ARMS RACE: Hundreds of thousand demonstrate against
nuclear arms. Gorbachev and Reagan agree to cut missile
arsenals 1987
ASSASSINATION ATTEMPT: President Reagan is shot by John
Hinckley and hospitalized 12 days
ADVERTISING: Promoted on larger scale than ever before
BEIJING: In China student-led pro-democracy demonstration in
Tiananmen Square is crushed by troops; heavy death toll

BERLIN WALL: The fall of communist government opens the
    Wall between East and West Germany in 1989. 74 persons
    had been shot during years the Wall stood. New era of
    German unity begins
BOMBINGS: Beruit: TNT-laden suicide terrorist in truck blows
    up Marine headquarters killing 241 Americans on peace
    making mission. A second truck bomb two miles away blows
    up French paratroop barracks, killing 58
COLD WAR: At Malta Summit Gorbachev in 1989 and President
    Bush affirm that the Cold War is over
DRUGS: International drug war, cocaine, crack, marijuana
EARTHQUAKE: San Francisco area: 67 killed, many injured,
    great property damage
ENVIRONMENT: Concerns: "Greenhouse Effect" ozone
    depletion, ocean dumping, acid rain, radon contamination,
    poor waste management and radiation leaks from nuclear
    facilities
EPIDEMIC: AIDS, racial tension, ecological abuse, violence,
    fear of violent attacks, disproportionate number of crimes,
    guns and drugs
FAMILY: Traditional and family values lessened, especially
    among young people. Moral fabric weakened although
    patriotism is strong and conservativism strengthened,
    surrogate parenting: "Baby M"
GOVERNMENT: Reganomics result in waves of economic
    recovery, new jobs, advocated low taxes, cutbacks in liberal
    social programs, military buildup, New York elects first
    black mayor
GRENADA: U.S. and Carribean forces invade Grenada: Marxist
    regime deposed
HOSTAGES: Iranian hostage crisis in Lebanon: 51 Americans
    held 444 days flown to freedom in 1981. U.S. agrees $8
    billion return to Iran in frozen assets. TWA flight 847 forced
    to land in Beruit, holding hostages 17 days. PLO hijackers
    seize Achille Lauro, an Italian cruise ship, and kill an
    elderly American
HURRICANES: Hugo pounds southeast coast and the
    Caribbean, kills 96 and leave much destruction

IRAN-CONTRA AFFAIR: Lt. Col. Oliver North involved in
     investigation, convicted of three felonies
OIL SPILL: Tanker Exxon Valdez strays off course, strikes reef,
     spills oil into Alaskan Coastline hundreds of miles
OLYMPICS: 1980 U.S. boycotts Moscow olympic games. In
     1984 Soviets boycott games in Los Angeles
ORGANIZATION: Guppies "God-fearing Urban Professionals"
PANAMA: Panama Canal handed over to Panama. Later, in
     1989, full scale invasion is made by U.S. because of
     corrupted government of Noriega, who flees, then surrenders
PALESTINE: PLO campaigns for independent Palestinian
     homeland. Leader, Yasser Arafat, challenges Israel
POLAND: Solidarity wins all but one seat in the first free
     election in 50 years
PERSIAN GULF: USS Vincennes erroneously struck
     commercial airliner of Iran in 1988, killing 290
SCANDALS: Department of Housing and Urban Dev. (HUD).
     Federal government bails out Savings and Loans. Pentagon
     papers
SOVIET UNION: In 1983 Soviets shoot down South Korean
     commercial airline, killing 269, which leads to world-wide
     condemning. Communism crumbles in Eastern Europe. In
     late 80's and Gorbachev leads toward freer society: glasnost
     (public accountability) and perestroika (economic freedom).
     1986 Accident at Chernobyl nuclear power plant: dangerous
     radiation, serious health damage
SPACE: Space shuttle Columbia completes its first flight, 1982.
     In 1986 Space shuttle Challenger explodes shortly after take
     off killing seven crew members. Space shuttle Discovery
     launches in 1989, three years after Challenger disaster
STATUE OF LIBERTY: Celebrates 100th birthday with 4 day
     extravaganza
TALK SHOWS: new popularity on radio and television
TERRORISM: From 1981 to 1986 there were 721 worldwide
     terrorism incidents with 2,122 deaths

Events and people of the 1990's:
PRESIDENTS: 1989 to 1993 George H. Bush
                          1993 William J. Clinton
VICE-PRESIDENTS: Dan Quayle and Al Gore
ABORTION: Parental notification upheld in Supreme Court.
    Supreme Court reaffirms Roe vs. Wade. Medical doctor is
    slain in antiabortion protest
AIR DROPS: U.S. begins airdrops of aid to Bosnia
BIBLE: Dead Sea Scrolls, rare Biblical documents, deciphered
    by computer
BOMBING: Blast shakes World Trade Center in New York
CABLE TV: FCC orders cuts in cable TV charges
CRASHES: Jet crash in neighborhood park in Colorado Springs,
    CO kills 25. Train derailment in Virginia injures 74
CULT: Religious cult in Waco, Texas standoff one month. 400
    Federal agents and local police mass near compound. Leader
    Koresh and 71 followers set fire to buildings and die
DEBATE: Anita Hill accuses Supreme Court nominee Clarence
    Thomas of sexual harassment, which unleashes strong
    debate. Senate confirms Thomas 52-48
EMPLOYMENT: Jobless rate in 1992 at five-year high. Senate
    passes Family Leave Bill for family emergencies
FERRY: capsizes in Haiti – hundreds lost at sea
FLOODS: In Mid West – one of the nation's worst national
    disaster. Flood loss more than $10 billion
GERMANY: East and West sign reunification treaty in 1990.
    East Germany apologizes for Nazi crimes and seeks relations
    with Israel
GOVERNMENT: First woman Attorney General: Janet Reno.
    President Clinton plans to curb campaign spending. He
    presents plan for gays in the military. Mrs. Hillary Clinton
    advocates Health Care program. Postage increased to 29
    cents for letters. Federal Reserves cuts interest rates in 1991.
    Supreme Court reaffirms school prayer ban claiming prayer
    is violation of separation of church and state
HOMOSEXUALS: Supreme Court in 1990 has ban on homo-
    sexuals in military. In 1993 objectors march in Washington
    D.C. In 1992 Colorado votes ban on Gay Rights law

HURRICANES: Devastates South Florida, razes thousand of
homes. Causes damage in other southern states. About 43
deaths. Devastates Hawaian Island Kauai. Cyclone in
Bangladesh kills more than 100,000. Nearly 8,000 U.S.
troops deliver food and medicine

I.R.A.: Fires at 10 Downing Street, home of England's prime
minister, in assault attempt. Also bombs two London rail
stations and crowded financial district killing 3, wounding 91

IRAQ: U.S. places embargo and sends troops after Iraq closes
Suez Canal

MEDICINE: Scientists find gene that causes cancer. Gene
therapy treatment of genetic disorders. Right to die upheld
for persons wishing cut-off of treatment for life-extension.
Safety of breast implants is questioned. DNA explored

MILITARY: U. S. drops aid to Bosnia which was fired on by
Serbs. Sarajevo market place slaughter by Serbs kills 66 and
wounds 200. U.N. forces win Persian Gulf War. General
Schwarzkopf leads. U.S. Air Force parachutes food, water
and medical supplies to refugees

PERSONALITIES: Rush Limbaugh, conservative commentator.
Ross Perot entered presidential race Oct., 1992. Tonya
Harding involved in assault against Nancy Kerrigan, 1994,
both Olympic skating stars. Former President Nixon dies

POLICE: Video records police beating black motorist Rodney
King in Los Angeles in 1992. Shown on TV, shocks the
nation. Four white officers acquitted. Violence erupts in Los
Angeles for three days. Death toll 50, property damage
millions

RUSSIA: Soviet communists relinquish power. New leadership
with Gorbachev as president. In July 1991 Boris Yeltsin
becomes president

SO. CALIFORNIA: Earthquake in early,1994 leaves 25,000
dwellings uninhabitable, traps many people, kills 16, col-
lapses freeways. Earlier brush fires in various areas devoured
almost 1,000 homes. Mud slides that followed later cause
great damage in Malabu area

SPACE: U.S. lands 53rd shuttle mission. Five astronauts aboard
     Columbia rescue 11 ton satellite. Telescope orbited into
     space on shuttle Discovery
STORMS: Heavy storm batters east coast and north, 6 ft. high
     snowdrifts. Tornados kill 25 near Chicago
SUDAN: Famine continues there and in other African countries
SUICIDE: Dr. Kevorkian assists suicide victims
THAILAND: 200 perish in factory fire
TRADE: U. S. trade deficit at 8 year low
TRIAL: Michael Griffin receives life sentence for shooting
     medical doctor abortionist. Lorena Bobbitt, not guilty of
     malicious wounding by reason of insanity for cutting off
     husband's penis
VATICAN: Pope visits Denver, CO for youth day program.
     Thousands attend
WHITEWATER: Federal Investigation of President Clinton's
     real estate venture and failed Savings and Loan